All Fired Up

All Fired Up

Kay Fulcher

The Holy Spirit lit the flame in the life of a
single mother in her thirties. These stories
reflect the difference between a life centred on
self and a life lived through the power, presence
and guidance of the Holy Spirit.

Zai Publishing

A catalogue record for this book is available from the National Library of Australia

I dedicate this book to my family:

To my parents: Lee and Audrey for giving me the greatest of gifts by loving each other and giving me a home filled with love and laughter.

To my three brothers: John, Bryan and Ross. You have given me nothing but happy memories.

To my daughter: Dimity. You are a gift from God that led me to God.

To my son by grace and marriage: Pete. You are a man who humbly walks with God.

To my grandchildren: Indiana, Lee, Peyton and Austin. You constantly fill me with delight. You make me so very happy...you know the rest.

Contents

Part One
The Fighting Spirit

And the disciples were filled with joy and with the Holy Spirit.

Acts 13:52

For the Spirit God gave us does not make us timid, but gives us power, love and self-discipline

2 Timothy 1:7

1
Learning to Fight

Was I born a fighter?

I came out feet first and took my first steps at nine months. I already had a two-year-old brother and two more brothers followed. Learning to fight was not optional. We all lived an outdoor adventurous lifestyle that included climbing trees, building cubby houses in the bush, yabbying in the local creeks, and hammering together our own go karts to race down the dirt roads. This love of outdoor activity transferred into a love for all sports, though unfortunately, it was not accompanied by any natural ability on my part.

Arthur Tighe, from across the road, would come over on a Saturday morning to watch boxing with my father. Arthur was a returned serviceman who had survived working on the Burma Railway as a Japanese prisoner of war. He was one of several returned soldiers living in our neighbourhood and his only son Trevor became one of my best friends. Arthur was a proud Indigenous man and, outwardly, did not bear the scars of his wartime ordeals. He was tall and thin and was an imposing presence wherever he went. Arthur seemed to always be full of cheer and cheek. I was allowed to sit and watch the boxing with Dad and Arthur as long as I did not make a sound.

My fascination with boxing has stood the test of time. It even extended to requesting a life size poster of Muhammad Ali as a bridesmaid gift when my brother got married, rather than the traditional jewellery usually afforded to the role. I read his autobiography, 'The Great One', written before he had even changed his name from Cassius Clay and I was impressed that he was so comprehensive in his training methods, including having exercises to strengthen every part of his body, even his big toes.

I don't think that was enough of a reason to explain all of the fights I had in primary school at Woodridge. Woodridge was a small village in the, then, Albert Shire Council. The South Coast railway line ran from South Brisbane to Tweed Heads between 1889 and 1964. Mail we received was always marked with, "Woodridge, South Coast Line." There was a small siding at Woodridge, built to pick up the locally harvested timber. My father was sent to teach there in what was a two-teacher primary school in 1954 when I was two years of age. My brothers and I had an idyllic childhood growing up "in the bush."

It is hard to understand why I had so many physical fights as a small child. Upon reflection, I thought it was because I had an older brother and hung out with him and the neighbourhood kids. They were almost all boys older than me. Perhaps there was a sense of compulsion to keep up with them, participating in any and all ventures without ever being accused of "being a girl". I know that I did not respect any boy who I could beat in a race or in a fight.

I was to be enlightened many years later by Mrs Moffatt, the mother of my childhood friend, Libby. Libby's family had a poultry farm and visiting her almost always included cleaning eggs at some stage. I walked past Libby's home every morning and afternoon on the journey between home and school. Several big mango trees stood in her front yard and Mrs Moffatt allowed us to pick them in season. One afternoon as she sat on her verandah, she witnessed several kids teasing me, calling me names and generally being bullies. She was about to go down and intervene when she saw me pick up a green mango, throw it straight and hard and hit one of the bullies squarely in the middle of their back. All of the bullies ran off and I continued on my way seemingly unperturbed. She told me that was when she realised that I could look after myself. That story made me understand that I was probably being teased a lot. I don't remember the teasing, but I do remember the fights.

Short, skinny, a basin haircut, a patch over one eye because of the laziness of the other and a face absolutely covered in freckles: all this provided plenty of ammunition for would-be teasers.

My best friend through primary school and into high school was Carolyn Wain. Carolyn's family ran a farm of dairy and mixed crops. Carolyn contributed a lot to the work that needed to be done on the farm. This included milking and churning butter by hand. Apart from her inherited attributes, Carolyn was fit and strong because of all of her physical endeavours. She could run as fast as any boy and throw the cricket ball further than anyone. Whilst I was the scrawniest, she was the tallest and strongest. Thankfully we were always on the same team. I was the organiser, and Carolyn was the gifted one, with all the talent and ability. However, we did compete in the classroom. We vied for the prized back-row corner seat that went to the student who came top of the class. I loved that spot because I could hide comics and books on the floor and keep myself otherwise occupied during the boring times in class. Having come top of the class, it was possible to get away with doing very little work as it was expected that you were doing everything you should. Needless to say, I didn't keep that spot despite having worked so hard to gain it, but then I would work even harder to get it back.

I only ever remember having one fight with Carolyn although I can't remember what it was about. Our teacher had sent us on an errand. All students loved the privilege of doing a job for the teacher outside of the classroom. We were probably arguing out the specifics of who would do what as we were going down the stairs. As we got to the bottom of the stairs, our interaction had moved on to pushing and shoving. I knew Carolyn was so much stronger than me. As she came in to hit me I somehow managed to get my leg behind her knee and trip her. She landed on the ground. Just then, a girl much older came down the stairs and saw Carolyn on the ground. She looked at me and said, "Why don't you pick on someone your own size!" We both just looked at each other and cracked up laughing. We never fought again.

Our Year Six teacher was Bob McLaren. We all loved him. He was young, tall and had a presence, which meant no one would dare disobey him. We all wanted to please him. We had parade every morning on the bituminised parade ground where we would line up in our classes and then march into class to piped music. My goal was to one day be the one who could choose the music to be played.

I was often late to parade because of making the most of every second of playtime. One day, as I scurried to get into line at the last minute, Larry Pouncey, stuck his foot out and tripped me and then menancingly laughed at my near fall. Larry and his family had recently arrived from England, and he was not a rough and tumble boy like the others in my class. I was shocked that he would trip me. However, without even thinking, I faced up to him with two left jabs followed by a right cross and he fell to the bitumen. At that moment I looked up to see Mr McLaren standing on the verandah with arms crossed, having observed the whole incident. I was worried all throughout parade as to what was going to happen to me.

We marched up to our classroom and as I passed Mr McLaren he motioned with his finger for me to go to him. Here we go, I thought. I hope I don't get the cuts.[1] As I approached him, he looked me in the eye and asked, "Who taught you how to box?" I said, "No one." That was the end of the incident. He never said another word about it. This caused me to ponder, how *did* I know how to box? I then remembered my Saturday morning ringside viewings with Dad and Arthur. I must have absorbed some boxing fundamentals without even realising it. Without coaches and physical education specialists in my childhood years, learning came more from observation and then from practice.

Our school had a netball team that won just about all of our matches. That was largely due to Carolyn's expertise as Goal Attack but also due to the fact that I organised practice sessions. I made sure the balls were inflated and that everyone turned up. We ran our own team, and the girls elected me captain. I played Centre and we spent a lot of time practising the centre pass. A female teacher came to school who was willing to train us, and we were very happy to have the support and interest. Up until then the only thing that seemed to matter in the school was boys' sport. Things turned sour pretty quickly. Miss Smith took an instant dislike to me. She said I was too short to play netball and not only took the captaincy from me, but removed me from the team and made me a reserve. I played very few minutes after that. To this day I do not understand her actions.

After practice one day Miss Smith asked all the girls what they wanted to do when they left school. She kept me until last and asked what I wanted to be. "I want to be a physical education teacher," I replied with no small amount of joy. Miss Smith looked at me and said, "You'll never make it." That was the end of the training session.

We were in our final year of primary school by then and one day, Miss Smith, who taught Year One, came to talk to our Year Seven teacher. They spoke on the verandah and then she went back to her classroom. My Year Seven teacher was my father and the best teacher I ever had. He said to the class, "Stand up all the girls who like Miss Smith." We universally did not like her and hence my great disappointment when every girl stood up except me. Two girls were chosen to go and help out in the Year One classroom. They were delighted of course, but when they arrived Miss Smith asked if everyone had stood up. "Yes, everyone except Kay."

Now they decided to be truthful! That made my already difficult relationship with her unbearable and I couldn't wait for the end of the year. I never regretted telling the truth, but it did make interaction with her even more awkward. I did not play netball again for twenty-five years.

Physical fights seemed to continue throughout primary school. I did get the "cuts" on the legs on occasion and I no doubt deserved it. The principal warned me that if I had one more fight I would be expelled. I remember thinking that if my father were not a teacher at the school, I probably already would have been expelled. It must have been embarrassing for him.

The end of physical fights came when I moved to high school, but here my love for sport and my competitive spirit was able to grow and be fostered. I travelled, by train, with my friends from Woodridge to Sunnybank for high school. Sunnybank was only in its third year and did not even have a senior class. Being so small, they had trouble fielding teams for Wednesday afternoon interschool sport. The captain of the softball team was a Woodridge girl, Rhonda Chapman. She knew of Carolyn's athletic ability and of my enthusiasm. So even though we were only in Year Eight, she asked us to join the school softball team. Neither of us had even seen a softball glove or bat but we eagerly joined. We loved the training.

I remember our first game was against Corinda State High. They were the biggest school in our zone and they were used to winning everything. They beat us eighty-three to nil. I don't know why the mercy rule was not invoked. However, rather than being deterred and embarrassed by the huge defeat, Carolyn and I were determined to learn and to get better. Each year the team improved. Unfortunately, Carolyn left school at the end of Year Ten. When I was in Year Eleven we had a really good team, with Sherry, a Year Twelve Canadian girl, who had lots of experience, as our captain. We also had two Year Ten girls who had gone to the same primary school and had played pitcher and catcher together for years. I played right field and was a consistent batter, usually getting safely to first base. In reality, I had no illusions about being anything other than the weakest player on the team.

Our first game was once again against Corinda, and we won easily. We were so overconfident that we went on to lose the next game. However, that was the last game we lost all season. We won our zone final against Corinda and then went on to play against the other zone winners for the Brisbane Premiership. We won our semi-final and then played Coorparoo in the Grand Final. It was a tight game and we took the field in the bottom of the last innings with a two-run lead. They had two out and two runners on base. Their pinch hitter came up to the plate and we all knew that this was going to decide the game, one way or another. She was a lefthander and soon the ball was flying over my head deep into right field. The base runners were advancing. I ran backwards trying to track the ball, but at some point, I lost it in the sun. I just stuck my hand up above my head to where I thought it might be and, to my astonishment, the ball stuck into my glove. The batter was out, and the advancing base runners did not score. We won the game! Our little school became Brisbane Premiers!

I still remember that moment even though it was over fifty years ago. The whole softball experience taught me to never give up, to persevere, train hard, and to keep learning because rewards will come.

Secondary school was all about sport for me. Softball and volleyball on Wednesday afternoons against other schools were the highlights of the week. I still organised equipment and was first to arrive and last to leave practices. I also lived for the inter-house athletics carnivals and the annual inter-house cross-country race.

In my last year of school, I won every athletic event except shot put. But that was not because I was such a good athlete. There were only nine girls in my senior year and only three of those had any interest in sport so, I determinedly entered every event to gain as many points as I could for my team. My goal in Year Twelve was to win the inter-house cross-country. I had come third and second in previous years and I wanted to leave a champion. I even did a bit of training running around our half-acre block. Winter was approaching and there had been no mention of the cross-country. I asked the organising teacher when it would be and he replied, "We are not having the cross-country this year." I was devastated. There was no explanation. I could not fulfil my ambition.

My final year of secondary school was a mixed bag. I have a lot of good memories as school was primarily fun.

However, my mother had suffered two miscarriages in the previous year and now she was unexpectedly pregnant again at age forty. She needed total bed rest for her pregnancy to have any chance of proceeding to full term. That left me, as the only girl, with a lot of responsibilities on the domestic front. The hardest part was getting off the train every afternoon and walking home, not knowing if Mum and the baby were still okay.

I was never one to spend much time on homework, just doing the bare minimum to get by. However, mathematics required more of an effort. Despite having topped the class in Year Eleven, I decided that maths had to go in order for me to cope. I could wing the other subjects with my memory and creative essay writing, but I could not wing maths. I stopped going to maths classes. This decision was made easier by the fact that we had a new graduate maths teacher. We had had the best teacher the year before but sadly, during the school holidays, our principal had died and our maths teacher, Mr Hall, was now acting principal. I remember this new teacher standing with his textbook open and not really knowing what he was talking about. He would ask a few of the boys to help him out. That annoyed me even more as I was the one who had come top of the class in Year Eleven, but he did not consider asking a girl. I decided he was a waste of space and never went back to class. Interestingly I was never missed and just went up to the prefects' room where I could complete my homework for the other subjects and then go home and focus on what had to be done there.

Mathematics was not the only class I decided to avoid in Year 12. The other was Religious Instruction.

It was not because I was not interested. In fact, it was quite the opposite. I started going to Sunday School before I had even started school and I loved it. I remember my very first Sunday school teacher, Doris Schodel. Mrs

Schodel taught me for my first two years. She seemed so old to me but, in reality, would have been in her forties. I remember the action songs she taught us, but most of all I remember that she always made me feel special and welcome. When I moved up to higher classes, Mrs Schodel did not forget me. In fact, she sent me a Christmas card every year until the day she died. That was forty years later. I was privileged to visit her before she died and to attend her funeral. I know that I was not that special and that she would have sent a Christmas card to every student she ever taught every year. I've never forgotten her.

I also remember my last Sunday school teacher, Jane Lowe. My friends and I were in Year Seven and Jane was a young nurse. We all thought she was so lovely. She even organised outings for us on days other than Sundays. As young girls going out without parents we felt so grown up. We would catch the train into the city and picnic at the Botanical Gardens. I was so impressed that Jane spent her own time with us outside of the official Sunday lesson. Later in life it was a pleasure to teach Jane's daughter. Both of these ladies left an indelible impression upon me, and it was such a joy to reconnect with them as an adult.

Leaving primary school and starting secondary school meant my peers and I were no longer in a Sunday school class. My friend, Patricia, and I decided we would like to become teacher's assistants. We loved helping out with the younger children. That was until we got a new minister who said we were too young to be teachers and had to go back into a class. We were no longer allowed to help with the younger children. We both left.

I had never lost interest in the stories of the Bible and so looked forward to these religious instruction lessons. I was always there, ready, first in line to go into class.

I remember the minister asking us to fill in a survey form. One question was to name your favourite book. My answer was, "The Bible." I was genuine as it truly fascinated me. I also asked a lot of questions in class because I really had an interest and a curiosity. I remember asking one day, "Is it possible to experience Heaven on Earth?" The teacher fobbed me off, but I was undeterred. That is until the next week, when I stood first in line ever so eager to go in. The minister came up to me and said, "And what strange questions are you going to ask of me this week?" I felt hurt and felt humiliated. I did not open my mouth in class. I did not hear a word he said. I just determined that I would never go back. And I didn't. My friend, Sue, and I would go to the sports' room, get out a volleyball net and ball and spend the Religious Instruction lesson playing volleyball. Nobody ever questioned what we were doing or where we should be. Our volleyball skills improved greatly.

2
Different Battles

For the next fifteen years I did not give God a thought. I knew He existed and believed all the teachings about Him. The Bible was still the most fascinating book I had ever read; I just didn't read it anymore. I believed in the Virgin Birth and the Resurrection. They just did not have any relevance to my life. In all of the years attending Sunday school, Church, Youth Group and Religious Instruction, there was never any mention about having a relationship with God.

I never remember any mention of the Holy Spirit. Personal salvation was not preached. The concept of everyone being a sinner in need of salvation was completely foreign to me. As I enjoyed my life into adulthood, I never considered myself to be sinful. I didn't think my life was radically different from any other young adult I knew exploring the freedoms in the seventies.

For those finishing secondary school in 1969, most could walk straight into a job with the economic rarity of full employment. I was trained in the use of the most up-to-date cash registers and worked in a local grocery store.

I was offered the position of supervisor, but only ever saw this work as a summer job to earn enough money to buy a car. Once I received my school results and realised that I had a scholarship to go to Teachers College for three years, the need for a car became more urgent. I bought my two-toned blue Hillman Minx for $320.00. After driving it to college for three years, I sold it for $300.00 and upgraded to an Austin 1800.

During these young adult years, two loves shaped my life.

My love of athletics continued after High School, and I joined Southern Suburbs Athletics Club. All events were enjoyable to me, but I had a particular passion for middle distance and long distance running. My first lesson again came from observation. I travelled by train twice a week to attend training sessions. When travelling by train into the city on a non-scheduled training day, I saw athletes training at my club's oval. I did not realise that athletes did extra training.

Just that one observation inspired me to read as much as I could about athletes and about coaching methods and then set my own schedule. I read books by Percy Cerutty, Arthur Lyiard, Peter Snell, Murray Halberg and Betty Cuthbert. Improvements started to come. The cross-country season invigorated me, and my training took place on the many bush tracks behind my house. At the end of my first cross country season, I was awarded a small trophy engraved, 'Best Trier.' That trophy still stays with me while almost all others have been disposed of.

By my second year I was selected to represent Queensland in the Australian Cross Country Championships. I had high hopes and continued to learn and train effectively. My times improved and I felt it was realistic to hope of one day representing my country.

Up until the 1980s, teacher training throughout Australia was primarily carried out in designated tertiary institutions called Teachers Colleges. Each year there would be athletic championships held in one of these designated colleges. I represented my college, Mt. Gravatt, in intercollegiate races. Mt. Gravatt was a very new and small college, and we were all excited to travel by bus from Queensland to Narrabeen, on the northern beaches of Sydney.

The longest distance at that meet was 800 metres, which was not my preferred event. However, it did lead in my mind, to my one and only *perfect* race. I had come second the year before to a woman who specialised in 800m races. Her gloating after that victory motivated me to spend time planning how to beat her the following year. I decided to sit in right behind her, breathe down her neck for the first five hundred metres and then, just as we entered the curve into the back straight, I would pass her with a quick turn of pace. I did not think she would react on the bend, as she would be so confident in her own ability to beat me. I basically sprinted from 300 metres out. I was so concerned that if I dropped off my speed even a little, she would catch me. I ended up winning by a large margin and broke the record, which thereafter stood for quite a few years. It was pleasing that the fight back, a year in the making had succeeded. This also convinced me, more than ever, that tactics and confidence play a huge role in winning races. I determined to keep on learning.

Whilst athletics was my focus, I also enjoyed a wonderful social life. I was surprised that some of my friends went out with the declared purpose of "meeting my husband tonight." I was going out to dance the night away and have fun. Marriage was not high on my list of goals. However, when I needed a partner for my college graduation ball, I knew that the place to go was Cloudland. Cloudland was a ballroom set high on a hill in the inner northern suburbs of Brisbane. This was a venue that not only had live bands, but also had a no alcohol policy. Girls would stand around the edges of the room and boys would file past, stopping to ask a girl to dance. I was brought up to always accept an invitation to dance. There I met John who was looking for a partner for his work's ball. The two balls ended up being on consecutive nights. John also loved to dance and soon became my first serious boyfriend. I remember him fondly. We had great dates with a lot of fun and many adventures. However, I did not love him and after nine months of dating, I wanted more. The night that I broke up with him, as I was walking into my house I was quite upbeat because he had accepted it so well. My exact thoughts were, "I hope all my break-ups are that easy." Looking back, that seems like a strange thing for a twenty-year-old woman to be thinking.

At the conclusion of my teacher training, students were guaranteed a job if they were bonded to the state education system for a time equal to the length of their training. Part of that agreement needed to be a willingness to go anywhere in the big state of Queensland. I was ready to leave home, ready for an adventure, now it was time to leave home and embrace independence. I applied to go to any of the places that, historically, graduates had not wanted to go, such as schools in the far north and far west of Queensland.

After our formal graduation, our celebration ball and subsequent after ball party, we did not sleep, we returned to our campus where every student's name was read out, accompanied by their placement. We sat on the floor eagerly awaiting our immediate future.

Imagine my shock when appointments were read out one by one and my placement was to be my own hometown, the school I had attended. Woodridge State Primary School. Not only had my brothers and I attended this school, my father had taught there and it was only two kilometres away from home. Some of my teachers were still there. It was hardly the place for me to establish my own identity. I was devastated.

Woodridge was no longer the small country school I had experienced. From a two-teacher school in 1954, it was now the largest primary school in the state, with over 1600 students. Woodridge had mushroomed during the late 1960s and early 1970s to be a high density, low socioeconomic housing area. It was no longer a farming area interspersed with bush to be explored. The growth happened very quickly once the Queensland government built thousands of housing commission homes for low-income families and developers promoted affordable house and land packages. There was not the necessary infrastructure or facilities to accompany the rapid increase in population.

Woodridge quickly developed a bad reputation for its high rates of crime. It was a place about which to be embarrassed. Most people would go out of their way to avoid driving through Woodridge and you would never get off a train at Woodridge station unless you really had to. Although I felt like we grew up in the bush, Woodridge, in reality, was only twenty-five kilometres south of the Brisbane GPO. When my appointment was read out as Woodridge, the disappointment was palpable. Now not able to leave home, my substitute act of rebellion was to buy a motorbike.

So Woodridge it was. There were buildings everywhere now and more being built. I started the year with forty-four students in Year Three. There were five Year Three classes in total. We ended the year with eight Year Three classes each still with over forty students; such was the continued rate of growth. My classroom was a temporary building with no blackboard. I still, however, remember it as a great year. I loved my class and fellow teachers and don't remember feeling stressed.

I do remember that in the last week of first term, the deputy principal, Brian Clark, came to my classroom accompanied by a man in a suit. That was an unusual sight! Brian introduced me to Hayden's father. Hayden was a lovely boy in my class. I started to scan my memory to think if I had done anything wrong regarding Hayden. To my surprise Hayden's dad said that they were leaving the area and that Hayden was very sad to be leaving his school. He was very happy and was having his best year. He wanted to come and thank me personally. I was shocked. After Brian escorted Hayden's dad away, he came back and said to me, "You need to treasure that. You won't get many of those". I didn't believe him. My thinking was that I have only been teaching one term, surely there will be many others. He was right. Such expressions of gratitude have been few and far between.

One of the positives of staying home and teaching at Woodridge was that I was able to continue my athletics training uninterrupted and compete every Saturday, either on the track or in cross-country races. I was chosen to represent Queensland for the second time and thrived on the experience. Looking back, it is hard to understand how this ambition could have come to a sudden halt. But it did.

Enter, the second love.

Meeting the man I will call Adrian, changed my life. After finishing my first year of teaching and having saved up $1000, I decided to buy a block of land and plan for a future where I would one day live by the beach. The Sunshine Coast was my favourite place. I especially loved the long, quiet isolated stretches of beach yet to be developed. However, when I went to the Courier Mail Real Estate section for the first time in my life I was taken by an ad for acreage in the Sunshine Coast Hinterland. My phone inquiry left me intrigued. Was it more to meet this man called Adrian than to see the land? He insisted that I bring my father with me because he didn't like to take young ladies on his own to inspect land. That seemed like a gentlemanly thing to do. I still remember what I wore, and it is a wonder that my father let me out of the house in such short shorts. Certainly that was not appropriate dress for walking around acreage properties.

I fell in love with the shake of hands. Physically, Adrian was my ideal man with his blonde hair, blue eyes, muscular build and charming personality. He was a confident extrovert; everything that I was not.

Even though I was the client, Dad sat in the front seat and I sat in the back for the two-hour drive. My eyes met with Adrian's in the rear vision mirror on more than one occasion. As we approached our destination, I was very taken with the rolling green hills around me. I remember rounding a bend and looking out to the left, thinking, "Wouldn't it be great if that was one of the blocks." At that exact moment Adrian declared that it was. This land became a part of my life for the next forty-five years. Adrian became a part of my life for the next ten.

Coming home from that outing, I was not thinking about the land, but thinking, "Now I know what my purpose in life is; to love Adrian." I really was willing to give up training sessions and even competition races to spend time with him. He became the focus of my life.

Our time together was always special, but in some ways the relationship was neither balanced nor healthy. I would stay home from training just in case he rang. Saturdays I spent with him driving around rural real estate developments rather than competing in athletic events. In fact, after meeting Adrian, I hardly ever competed seriously again. It is hard to imagine that I could have so easily replaced my love of athletics, together with all of my dreams and ambitions, for the love of a man.

The day before I met Adrian, I had received a transfer to Murgon State School from the commencement of the school year in 1974. We had six weeks of getting to know each other and of cementing our relationship, before I finally left home and drove to Murgon. The major complication was that the beginning of 1974 saw southeast Queensland suffer the worst flooding in more than one hundred years. The start of school was delayed for one week because of the extensiveness of the floods and the difficulties of travel.

I set off in my second-hand Austin 1800. The marketing slogan for this vehicle was, it *floats on fluid*. I soon found that did not apply to flood waters. A trip that would usually take no more than four hours, took me eight hours with many a detour around challenging creek crossings. It was late afternoon when I was very close to Murgon and heard a change in the sound of the engine and observed a red light come on the dashboard. The car and I limped into a petrol station on the outskirts of town. Remarkably, being a Sunday, there was a mechanic on duty. The diagnosis was a destroyed fan belt. Apparently replacing this on an Austin 1800 was not a straightforward task. It was some hours later and in full darkness that I arrived in town and went to check in to the Australian Hotel. To my surprise, the hotel was locked and there was no one in sight. My father and I had driven to Murgon during the school holidays in an attempt to find accommodation. Being unsuccessful, he assured me that I would find somewhere to live once I got to the school and met the staff.

There was a public phone box in the main street so I went there to phone the hotel in the hope that someone would answer. It was the days of a manual exchange and when I asked for the hotel the operator replied, "There will be no one there at this time on a Sunday night." After telling her that I was booked in for the night, she said that she would ring the owner and that he would come and open up the hotel for me. So, in less than twenty-four hours, I discovered that leaving home was not all fun and games.

I was shown to a small room with a bed and a wardrobe. When I opened the wardrobe, the door hit the bed. That's how small it was. The mosquitos were so bad that I thought they would pick me up and carry me away but, being exhausted, I drifted off to sleep. Only to be woken up by late night drinkers who decided to gather under the verandah and continue to party through the night. I can assuredly say that up to that point in my life, this was the worst night ever. As I left the hotel to walk to school, I declared that I would not spend another night there and would sleep in my car if I had to. Thankfully, I met Beth, a fellow novice to the school, who was looking for a flatmate. Beth was newly engaged and her fiancé lived in Brisbane. I was in love with Adrian and he lived in Brisbane. Beth and I travelled together every weekend to spend time with the men in our lives.

Despite wanting to leave home and have adventures in a country town, I did not give the town a chance because my heart was never there. I loved my class and the children in it but was always thinking of my next trip to Brisbane. At the end of that year, I was able to obtain a transfer to a school in Redcliffe, a city just to the north of Brisbane. This allowed me to find accommodation on the north side of Brisbane only twenty minutes away from Adrian. Despite the challenges of teaching in three different schools in three years, I loved my vocation. School was a place of enjoyment and Adrian and I were both very committed to our careers. Whilst serving my three years with Education Queensland, I was also studying part-time to complete a degree; this time specialising in Health and Physical Education. Now I was able to fulfil my childhood dream of becoming a physical education teacher.

I obtained a position at Lourdes Hill College, a Catholic boarding school situated on a hill on the southern bank of the Brisbane River. It was now 1976 but the girls were still wearing bloomers under their sport uniforms and modesty seemed far more important than any sporting ability or achievement. One of my roles was to cater for 800 girls participating in sport or recreation on a Thursday afternoon. This meant that almost every teacher needed to be involved in supervising an activity. Most were in no way keen. However, there was a young man on a teacher exchange from England and he was super keen. He wanted to take a group of girls for *soccer*, so this sport was eagerly added to the list of options.

The day after the list of options was distributed to the students, I was summoned to the principal's office. Sister Bridget stood and pointed to a sheet of paper on her desk.

"This word!" she said, "Girls should not even see this word."

I looked down at the sheet of paper thinking that I must have made a typing mistake and somehow ended up with a rude word on the paper. The offensive word was soccer. I had to recall all of the lists, destroy them and make a new list that did not include such an "offensive suggestion".

Things did change over the seven years I was at Lourdes Hill. I loved my time there, made lifelong friends and certainly grew professionally. Much of this growth and enjoyment was due to my co-worker, Enid. Enid proposed that we make use of the river that formed the boundary of the school property. She instituted a system whereby students built sailing boats and learned how to sail. I undertook training as a canoe instructor and instituted canoeing as part of the Physical Education curriculum. These activities led to many great camps and adventures.

The other major focus of my time there was aquatic, swimming, lifesaving and kayaking. These classes and associated activities required a lot of extra hours of commitment. However, this was an endeavour to which I was very devoted and never resented any extra time commitment.

Adrian was a workaholic, more devoted to the money he could make than to the actual work process. However, he was very good, firstly at selling, then managing and ultimately developing. He had a charismatic personality and had a gift of motivating others to do their very best. Our time together was usually not spent in socialising with others. We valued our joint solitude and loved visiting isolated beaches and going on adventures in his four-wheel drive. We relaxed together and it was like our lives melded together. We never argued. We just enjoyed each other.

However, it was not a traditional relationship. He had two children from a previous marriage and had experienced a bitter divorce. He did not want to go down that path again. I accepted that, and was happy with what we had. My friends could not understand. "He's not going to marry you. So why don't you find someone else who will?" Again with the marriage obsession! Marriage was not the end goal of my being.

After five years, I discovered that he was being unfaithful with a woman at work. She was moving interstate and, as a parting gift, she decided to let me know what had been going on. I was devastated. I ended the relationship; so hurt that I was numb. He begged forgiveness and wanted me back. I had no intention of going back. He persisted and persuaded me to meet him. I didn't turn up. He didn't give up. I can't even remember why I took him back. It took several months, and I realised that I still did love him and did not want anyone else.

I was confident in our relationship when we reunited and had genuinely forgiven him. I felt comfortable enough to suggest that we think about having a baby. I had always wanted a large family and remember sketching house plans with enough bedrooms to accommodate many children. I also remember choosing names for the boys and for the girls. I couldn't imagine life without children. Adrian wasn't against the idea but suggested that we wait two more years. Those years went very quickly, and his next response was, "Let's save another ten thousand dollars so we can really celebrate. Two more years?"

After those two years were up, I was about to turn thirty and really did not want to wait any longer. Adrian agreed and I went off the pill. I was filled with joy in anticipation of becoming pregnant with his child. However, what I expected to be an exciting time of anticipation became a time of unexpected confusion.

His behaviour changed markedly, and this had the effect of making me remember the devastating time of his affair many years earlier. I was confused and did not want to believe that my suspicions could be correct. I did not need to do much investigating as he openly admitted that he was involved with a woman from his daughter's swimming club. I don't know what shocked me and hurt me the most: his affair or his thinking that it would make no difference to us. As far as I was concerned, this was the end of "us". I immediately decided to leave. I already owned my own home and I put that on the market, as I knew that I had to physically move away from him and start life afresh on my own.

While waiting for the settlement of my house, I stayed with my mother who still lived in Woodridge. I was then able to put in my resignation and complete the school term. My father had died just two years previously and I really missed his presence in my life, especially at this time.

I still had the land that I had bought ten years previously; from Adrian on the day we met. There was nothing there.

I had planted over one hundred trees and had camped there on a few occasions, but it was basically eleven acres of scrub. One thing that made this upheaval more bearable was the acquisition of a very special dog. Going to the country to live alone, made me think about the need to get a dog. I was offered a job as a swimming coach in a town close to my block of land. This made my move to the country a certainty. One afternoon as I drove into my mother's back yard there was a blue heeler just sitting there. Mum didn't have a dog. Where did she come from? Mum described how she just turned up and had refused to leave and how all inquiries to find the owner had failed. Just then she jumped into the back of my Hilux Ute. Here was the dog I envisaged. I called her Magic. We started a great partnership.

I had a double garage erected on the land and Magic and I started a new adventure. I had a camp stretcher, a portaloo,[2] a two-burner camping stove and a kerosene lantern. There was no township, just an area called Carters Ridge. No neighbours were visible from my property, but I soon got to know a few families in the area who were very supportive of this single city girl who did not know what she was doing. I would get a supply of fresh water from the swimming pool where I worked mornings and afternoons. This also allowed me to have showers. I had dams constructed in two of the gullies on the property and from one of them I pumped water up to a tank near the shed. Although I did not yet have fresh rainwater, I had water for gardens and washing. Despite these circumstances, I don't remember feeling emotionally distraught.

I hadn't been feeling well but I assumed that was because of the stress and exhaustion of packing and moving. However, my vague feeling of being unwell, turned to suspicious nausea and vomiting. That was especially prevalent in the mornings. I could not even keep water down. I then remembered that I had not had a period since leaving Adrian and began to consider that I might be pregnant.

One of my wonderful neighbours recommended an obstetrician in the nearby town of Nambour. Nambour was the biggest town in the Sunshine Coast region. There was a quite large public hospital as well as a private hospital. After the pregnancy was confirmed, I decided to see a private doctor for the first six months and then transfer to the public system. Not only was I starting a completely new life, I was going to be a mother and have the baby that I had been longing for.

I didn't feel that I could meet Adrian face to face. I'd had no contact with him since leaving, so I decided to write him a letter to inform him of the pregnancy. I expressed my joy and requested that if he could not share my happiness, then perhaps he should stay away. He did drive up to see me and said that he was happy for me. However, he did not want to be involved. I was glad at least that he was not negative. I had expected to go it alone and was always going to be thrilled to be on this journey of motherhood.

Towards the end of my first trimester, I began to experience severe abdominal pains in my left side and began to bleed. I was able to drive the forty minutes to Nambour to see my doctor. After examining me, he called in his colleague. They both diagnosed an ectopic pregnancy. This diagnosis was confirmed with a scan. I was confused and didn't understand the ramifications of their diagnosis. That was when my doctor seemingly callously said, "We will either suck the foetus out of your tube or we may have to cut out the tube." While he didn't seem concerned because, I "had another tube," I sat there thinking: You are talking about my baby.

By now it was late Friday afternoon and the instructions were not to go back to the shed where I had no phone. I could not be alone because a life-threatening haemorrhage was a possibility. So, I was ordered to have bed rest for the weekend. I stayed with neighbours who lived about two kilometres from me. They had inside plumbing and a phone. My mother drove up from Woodridge to stay with me. Whatever procedure necessary was booked in for first thing Monday morning at Selangor Private Hospital. I was in a state of shock. I could not accept the diagnosis, or the projected outcome. For the first time in fifteen years, I prayed to God.

3
Losing to Win

During the weekend of prescribed bed rest, I prayed The Lord's Prayer that I had learned as a child. My cry to God was, please save my baby! Lying there in a state of shock, I could not even consider the consequences if the doctors were right. Numbness took over my body and my brain. At some point, I had a vision of a perfect little baby girl coming out of my abdomen. From that moment on I had hope. More than hope, I believed that God had answered my prayer.

The Monday morning appointment at the hospital was kept. I still had a sense of calmness, even as they sent me for another scan before the proposed surgery. There seemed to be quite a bit of confusion and consultation among the medical staff.

Finally, the surgeon actually addressed me, the patient, and said that the pregnancy was not ectopic, but that the foetus was exactly in the womb where it should be, not in the tube. Relief flooded over me. I knew God had done what was, medically, impossible to do. After that I never stopped praying. The Lord's Prayer became part of my daily routine as I now joyfully prepared to be a mother to a little girl.

I contacted Adrian to give him the update but that was the last time I spoke to him until two weeks after the birth of my precious daughter, Dimity.

He rang to ask, "What did you have?" Once he knew everything went well, he did not continue contact.

During this time, the practicalities of life remained difficult. However, I received a lot of support from locals, some of whom I had not previously known. One couple in particular was so helpful. I knew from the start that they were Christians. I think at that stage I probably considered myself to be a Christian. They would bring me eggs and produce from their garden, invite me over for meals and call in to see if I needed anything. Clearly, I did need a lot of help, never having managed a generator before and being completely clueless about petrol pumps, kerosene fridges and managing an acreage property. Thinking back, it seems strange that they never invited me to church nor talked to me about their beliefs. They just loved me.

As the birth approached, I became more and more excited about what was going to be the most precious time of my life. Despite attending a few prenatal classes, I was totally unprepared for a difficult birth. I knew I was a fighter and thought I could handle anything. How wrong can you be? After twenty-six hours of exhaustion and pain, I remember thinking: Just knock me out and give me the baby tomorrow.

Throughout my pregnancy, on every visit to the Nambour Hospital I had received a good report. These visits were in small cubicles with no real sense of actual privacy. One female doctor always seemed to be gruff with her patients and I was actually a bit scared of her. The random system of patient care meant that I never saw her in any of my visits and I was grateful.

Halfway through my labour in walked Dr June. The presence of this doctor who, actually scared me, did not help my level of stress. I had already received an injection of pethidine but requested more. My request was denied. Then the decision was made to rupture my waters. This did not worry me, as I was not expecting any pain. Wrong again. After the procedure I was gasping, more in shock than in actual pain.

Dr June's gruff response was, "Get over it. It's not still hurting is it?"

June was meant to finish her shift at 10pm and I am forever grateful that she stayed for the birth of my precious daughter. What she seemed to lack in bedside manner and empathy, she more than made up with expertise. I later found out that Dr. June's birthday was June 19, the day of my long labour. Part of the reason she stayed on was the hope that this baby would be born on her birthday. However, Dimity waited until 20 minutes after midnight to arrive on June 20.

At the point of exhaustion, I was ready to give up when June held up the forceps. To me they looked like giant kitchen tongs.

As she waved them in front of my face she said, "Look at these. Do you want these shoved up you? It's no good for you and it's no good for the baby. Now push!"

I pushed. Dimity was born and my life changed forever. As I held her in my arms, nothing else mattered.

June immediately became like a different person as she began to stitch up the damage. She spoke like she actually cared, and the conversation led us to the realisation that we had a very close mutual friend, Enid, from my days at Lourdes Hill. From that moment on she treated me like a friend and had extra special care and interest in Dimity. As she stitched, she was tutoring the intern who had come to replace her. He had never stitched a woman before. I was shocked to see the women who gave birth under his care hardly able to walk the next day. Whereas June's expert needlework meant I had no discomfort whatsoever. Ironically, Dr. June turned out to be a very special lady.

Arriving home from the hospital and facing the solo responsibility for my little girl was completely overwhelming. My brother, Bryan and his wife Michelle, picked us up from hospital and stayed the first night. Then I was on my own with my newborn daughter. Two great friends, Maree and Gabrielle came to spend time with me in those early days and their help was monumental. Nevertheless, this amazing time of motherhood brought both joys and struggles not before experienced. Lack of sleep, over supply of milk and accompanying mastitis, not eating well, coping without power and without other adult interaction, all meant that every day and every night was a stretch in some way. However, these challenges did not dim the joy of motherhood and the two of us set about having adventures that would continue for the next two decades.

The one constant in our lives was The Lord's Prayer. It was prayed daily, together with a plea for God to get us through the next day. He always did.

I wanted to stay at home with Dimity for as long as possible. After selling my car and replacing it with a far lesser machine; selling my antique furniture; cashing in my life insurance and my superannuation, I had reached the end of my resources and had to go back to work. Dimity was fourteen months old and I was pleased to find a lovely family day care mum to care for her. The job meant moving to Brisbane and leaving our little piece of paradise. It also meant that we had interaction with family and friends, plus other benefits to make life more rewarding.

Kerrie was my teaching partner at my new school and was very overtly a Christian. I actually thought of her as being a bit too religious but that was balanced out by the authenticity of her faith and her genuinely godly nature. I thought that Kerrie was being very nice when she invited me to church. I never seriously thought about going, but it was nice to be asked.

One Sunday Kerrie and her husband Keith, invited Dimity and me to go bike riding in the City Botanical Gardens followed by a picnic. I did think it was unusual that they were not going to church. However, I later found out that they were going to an evening service. We had a lovely day and they invited us back to their place for dinner. They also invited us to go to the youth service at their church that evening. It had been a long day and I fully expected that Dimity would be tired and whingey and that I would have the perfect excuse not to go. Dimity, however, was in fine spirits after dinner and there was no easy way out. I decided we would go, keep them happy and that would be the end of that. God had other ideas.

My Father had died almost two years before Dimity was born. We were always very close and I missed him dearly. As well as saying The Lord's Prayer every day, another one of my survival strategies was to sing his favourite song every night in the shower. Dad generally did not come to church with us, except at Christmas. He loved to sing and his favourite carol was 'It Came Upon the Midnight Clear.' He was always disappointed that they would sing it to a different tune. It had become a family Christmas tradition to sing this song to Dad's tune. Singing that song made me feel close to him and think of how supportive he would have been had he still been alive.

So here I was in church for the first time in seventeen years. It was April and the whole church was standing up singing 'It Came Upon the Midnight Clear' to Dad's tune. I felt as if I had come home. I remember everything about that service. The testimonies from the youth and the youth leaders impressed me greatly. The sermon from John Chapter Ten spoke to me directly. It was like I was the only one in the building and God was speaking personally to me.

For some reason these words especially impacted me:

"His sheep follow him because they know his voice. I have other sheep that are not of this sheep pen. I must bring them in also. They too will listen to my voice, and there shall be one flock and one shepherd."[3]

I went home and found my grandmother's Bible and started reading it. I have never stopped.

4
Hearing God's Voice

After having been cajoled into going to church the first time, I did not need any persuasion to go back the next week and for every week after that. I had concerns about how a single mother and her child would be received but these were allayed when a family invited Dimity and me back for lunch that first Sunday morning. I absorbed the preaching and the words of the hymns. I remember being surprised that the congregation was singing 'Amazing Grace.' This song had hit the Top 40 in my late teens and, much to my surprise, Dad had bought the record. I had no idea it was a Christian song. Because Dad liked it and played it, there was no way to pay any teenage attention and still think of myself as being "cool."

Three church occasions stand out as determining the future course of my life. The first was when the pastor suggested that he might see me again at the night service. I thought, "Why would anyone go to church twice on one day?" For some reason, I recalled the shock of seeing athletes training on days other than scheduled club days and realising that if you wanted to be a serious athlete you needed to train, not only more than twice a week, but often more than once a day. If I were to be serious about being a Christian then, of course, I would go back to church at night.

The second shock came months later when from the pulpit came the words, "Those of you who are Christian and those of you who are not…" I didn't hear anything after that. My feathers were ruffled. What does he mean? Surely everyone there was a Christian. Was I a Christian? What was this? Was there some initiation ceremony? My frustration rose. I felt like shaking my friend Kerrie and demanding that she tell me, "How do you become a Christian?" Kerrie gave me a little tract entitled, 'Knowing God Personally.' After reading that, digesting the information, kneeling down and praying the prayer, I can truly testify to being Born Again. I could not remember the last time I had actually felt *happy*.

I had been in survival mode, and in that mode, my emotions were usually shelved, being too difficult to navigate. Now I felt like I had fallen in love, only this time it was pure, unselfish love. The accompanying empowerment made me feel like I could walk through walls if I had to.

Accompanying my twice-weekly church attendance was a renewed thirst to read the Bible and to improve my understanding. I was so determined to turn my life around and to do whatever God was asking of me, that I would rise an hour earlier than Dimity to read through the New Testament and identify any commands.

The third event came during a half-night of prayer. I had never been to a prayer meeting before, let alone a four-hour prayer meeting. The first meeting was focused on World Missions. There were only a handful of people, but it seemed everyone else except me had this astounding knowledge of what was going on in specific parts of the world. They knew of political situations, economic struggles and even the names and circumstances of missionaries globally. I stayed in silence the whole hour. On the one hand, impressively blown away and on the other hand feeling totally inadequate. I remember thinking at the end of the hour, God if you ever ask me to go anywhere, I will go.

The next hour was devoted to praying for the annual District Conference. The Wesleyan Methodist Church operated through a representative structure. Each year there would be a conference where equal numbers of ministerial and lay candidates would represent their local church. District leaders would give reports of the year's activities. There were also business sessions where motions could be moved, debated and voted upon. Elections were held for district leaders and the appointment of pastors to local churches for the coming year was ratified. This was known as the stationing sheet. At this stage I knew very little about a district conference. All I knew was that it was for leaders and therefore nothing to do with me.

As people began to pray for the conference, I was still thinking about missions. Then for the first time, came an experience of hearing God's voice. He said, "Go to Conference." I immediately recognised this as God speaking because there was no way for that thought to have come from me. My response was immediate. "No. God you misunderstood. I meant I would go anywhere on the mission field." Nonetheless I started to tune in to the prayers.

I soon learnt that the conference was not just for church leaders. Many people went with their families as part of their annual holidays. They would camp or stay in cabins and catch up with people from all over the state. I also learnt that there were programs running throughout the conference for children and that there would be a guest speaker from the United States at the evening rallies. It was to be held in the September school holidays. As we had no plans, I decided we could, in fact, go. So I borrowed a tent, and Dimity and I went to our first ever district Conference.

As we drove into Warwick looking for the campsite, I got lost for the first time in my life. Warwick is a town of about 15000 people, 150 kilometres southwest of Brisbane. It is a significant town serving the farming district known as the Darling Downs. There is a Christian campsite there, Kingswood Park and for many years this was the venue for the Queensland District Conference of the Wesleyan Methodist church. We ended up getting to the campsite just on dusk. It was a challenge in near darkness to put up the tent that I had never used before and a tired four-year-old was not really helpful. Many people walked past but no one offered to help this struggling small family. I felt very much out of place and unwelcome. Not experiencing any better hospitality during dinner, I decided that we would stay the night and go home in the morning. Some months earlier, a team from Kingsley College had visited our church. I was so impressed with their ministry and their testimonies and had even thought that going to Kingsley was perhaps something I could do one day. Now I was thinking, you don't belong here and you would not belong at Kingsley.

I was prepared to leave even before breakfast. However, our neighbouring campers, Kay and Mike Tilley came over to say how glad they were that we were there and would we sit with them at the service? That was enough for me to stay until after the service. The guest speaker was Don Polston from the United States. I remember that he related that more "mature" Christians sometimes squash the enthusiasm of young Christians. He encouraged me to listen to God and to not be dissuaded from His purposes.

As a result of his message, we stayed for the week, and for many years after that, going to the annual conference was one of the highlights of our year. I came home from that first conference with a renewed intention to go to Kingsley College one day. For the second time I heard God's voice, "Go next year."

It was now October. Dimity was not yet at school. I had bought a house. How could we possibly go next year? I proceeded to face all of these obstacles one by one. Dimity was able to start school in Melbourne if she turned five before the end of June. She was going to turn five on June 20. I put the house on the market and it sold the next day. I asked and was granted a year's leave from the Education Department.

We were going to Kingsley. The plan was to learn as much as I could in one year and hopefully become a better mother and a better teacher.

The journey to Kingsley was a road trip of nearly two thousand kilometres. I can't look into the mind of a four-year-old leaving behind all that she knew. Although I knew that Melbourne was so far away, and that we would be on the road for close to three days, Dimity had no concept of these times and distances. The first stopover was exciting, with a swim in the motel pool and, rare for us, a meal out at their restaurant. However, most of the second day was interspersed with tears and the same question, "Whose idea was it for us to go to Melbourne?"

I had no idea of what to expect from our home for the next year, other than it was a two-bedroom flat on campus. When we arrived on the third day of travel we were met by our neighbours and a little girl called Rainbow, before we even got out of our car. It was to be the people on campus that made our life extraordinary. In fact, it was the thought of community life that had held most concern for me, having in recent years, lived such an independent and, in many ways, isolated life. Yet living amongst families, singles, lecturers and staff from many different cultures was a complete joy. Such a life was not without challenges however.

Every student was required to have a Christian service appointment. Mine was to be a Sunday school teacher at Broadmeadows. It was held in the afternoons and it was organised by a very dedicated local doctor and her son, who were part of the college church congregation. In some ways, Broadmeadows mirrored the Woodridge that I had wanted to escape from many years earlier. It was a low socioeconomic area with a high density of social housing and a high crime rate. A bus would travel around the streets of Broadmeadows on a Sunday afternoon and pick up the children. They would come from the streets or from their front yards just as they were. The bus would arrive at the hall and children would climb out of its windows, over the roof of the bus and in and out of the hall windows. Coming from well-organised and disciplined classrooms, this first experience of meeting the children I was to teach left me in a state of shock.

Before breaking up into classes, I sat down with Dimity for the communal singing and noticed the girl in front of us had head lice crawling in her unkempt hair. I sat there and actually thought: I hope she is not in my class. I soon thanked God that Samantha was in my class and that I got to visit her at home and meet her family. I was shocked by my own prejudices and thankful that God had given me the opportunity to grow in grace. Life lessons more often occurred outside of the classroom than within it. I became very much aware of just how much more I had to learn and continue to be transformed by these experiences.

Years later, Dimity questioned why I took her to Melbourne for three years to be teased by boys. Despite this complaint, these years provided us both with great friendships and experiences that shaped our future lives. Yes, the planned one year did turn into three.

5

God Continues to Speak

My goal was to learn as much as I could, not to gain a specific qualification, but to become a better and more knowledgeable Christian. I did not even know that there were different translations of the Bible, so I certainly had a lot to learn. During the first semester I completed all of the first year subjects and a couple of extra ones. As second semester was being planned, there was a day on which I had no classes. I did not want to waste any of my time so explored all possibilities.

The only subject I could take on that spare day was "Evangelistic Preaching". I had not even completed "Introduction to Preaching" and never had any intention of opening my mouth in church. However, there was no official prerequisite so, rather than have a spare day I enrolled for this subject not really knowing what it was all about.

The first class saw me in a room filled with experienced male preachers. They were either fourth-year students or already qualified pastors enrolled for professional development. So out of place did I appear that the Lecturer came to me during break to ask if I thought I should really be doing this subject. This question actually did the opposite of deterring me. He then conceded to allow me to continue with the class because I was a teacher and used to speaking in front of a class. The class required preaching three evangelistic sermons. One was to be peer-reviewed in class and two others had to be in real life situations. As I was preparing one of the messages I again heard the voice of God: "Preach the Gospel to the Poor."

My reaction was twofold:

1. Evangelist preaching was just an academic exercise.

2. I can't preach. I am a woman.

The second was never actually stated, nor a factor in my being discouraged. However, I had read in 1st Timothy about women not being permitted to teach. Although I had several female lecturers, one of whom was an Ordained Minister. I did not see any conflict there but I was so determined to obey every instruction and not act in opposition to God's will. So that caused me to sincerely questioned this call. After studying this passage in context and in comparison with other passages where women were active in ministry. I felt confident in accepting God's call on my life. This study together with my sermon preparations and deliveries served to confirm God's call on my life. I am certainly grateful that I belonged to a denomination that had always ordained women.

I resigned from Education Queensland and committed to stay at Kingsley College to complete a Bachelor of Theology. I was most concerned about telling my mother that we would be staying longer. Mum had started going to church after my baptism and since my leaving had continued to faithfully attend. My news to her was received with this answer, " I'm not surprised. We had a missionary speaker this morning and I felt that you would be a missionary one day." God had indeed gone before.

My Christian service appointment in second year was to an inner-city church working with the elderly. This was a widely diverse group of people. There were those who had lived in the same terraced house their whole lives in what had been a working class area and there were those newer to the area who had moved into a now trendy suburb. I had the privilege of visiting each in their homes and of organising weekly meeting, activities and outings.

In my first year of college I attended the Glenroy church in the mornings and I had met a lady called Rita. Rita stood out as being a bit different from the other ladies. She always walked with her head down and I don't think I ever saw her smile. She was faithful in her attendance and in her assistance whenever there was a need. I wondered if she had any friends as I saw no evidence of it. So I decided to ask Rita if she would like to come with me each Thursday as I travelled across the city to our senior's meetings. Having accepted my invitation Rita and I participated in the first of many games days. Rita was very quiet and did not interact with the others. I expected no more. As I parked outside of Rita's home after the outing, she did not get out of the car. This conversation followed.

I recognised that lady called Hilda. After my father came home from the war he could not handle the noise of us kids around the house. During Summer, my brother and I were sent to the pool every day. I was a very naive teenage girl and I met a man there who took advantage of me. I became pregnant. When my father found out he packed a suitcase and kicked me out of home. I ended up in a Salvation Army Home for wayward girls. We were treated very badly. Every morning at 5am a bell would ring and we would have to get up, go outside and shower in cold water. We were told that this was punishment for our sin. When my baby was born all I know is that I had a girl but

I never got to see her or hold her. I don't know what happened to her. The woman who rang the bell and took us out for showers was Hilda. I will never forget her face.

I was shocked at the story but also shocked at Rita's seeming lack of emotion. She was not angry with Hilda. In fact she still believed that she deserved to be treated that way. Rita went on to describe how to this day she would scrub herself in the shower until she bled, hoping to wash the dirtiness out of her life. We had a beautiful time talking about the blood of Jesus and it's cleansing power. I was also able to share how I was a single mother, but I was a single mother by choice and not because I was a victim of abuse. Jesus loved us both equally and it was His purposes that we meet.

Rita was happy to keep coming every Thursday and Hilda remained oblivious to who she was. I continued to visit Rita and it was a great joy when I began to see her walk along the road with her head held high. This whole encounter served to remind me that God knows every detail of every person's life and that He can and does orchestrate circumstances that bring about healing. Rita and I kept in touch until she died and she encouraged and supported me in all I did.

I had taken God's call to preach as a call to overseas Mission and I remember standing at the sink washing up and saying to God, "I will go anywhere in the world." The reply was instant: "Go to Woodridge."

"No God. I meant that I would go anywhere in the world except Woodridge."

It was now fifteen years since I graduated as a teacher and asked to go anywhere in the state, only to end up in Woodridge. This couldn't be happening again. I was ready to go anywhere in the world, ready for an adventure and

God said, "Go to Woodridge." I know that message could not have come from my brain. I never told anyone that I had once lived in Woodridge and that my mother still did. It was the hometown of which I was very ashamed. I'm not sure that I would have done anything about that call from God had it not been confirmed to me during the following two weekends.

As I was about to enter my final year of college, I felt totally inadequate to do what God had called me to do, "Go to Woodridge." Even though it was literally the last place on Earth I wanted to go, I decided to write my thesis on how you would plant a church in Woodridge, if you were going to do so. A Baptist Pastor called Paul was in some of my classes. He was a church planter who had planted churches in Queensland and was now pastoring in a large rural town fifty kilometres north of Melbourne, called Bacchus Marsh. After speaking with Paul, I went to the principal to ask if my final Christian Service Appointment could be working with Paul as his intern for a year. It was unheard of to complete Christian Service Appointments with other denominations. However, permission was granted and so began a formational year.

I was not a Baptist, did not live in Bacchus Marsh, and was quite obviously a woman and yet the church accepted me as their Assistant Pastor for this one year. Paul initially took me with him on pastoral visits and then allowed me to venture out on my own. I was able to visit all families, sit and talk, pray, hang out the washing, vacuum or whatever the need was at the time. Preaching once a month stretched me, particularly when I could not choose my own passages but had to preach on the passages given to me. Everything was preparation for ministry, including attending business meetings and praying with Paul and observing him and his family. The people of this church accepted and loved my daughter and me. They believed in me and supported me when I left. Some stayed in contact for over thirty years.

Once a term I travelled with my daughter to the Gippsland area of Victoria to the township of Yarram. It is a beautiful town of just over 2 000 people. National Parks and beautiful beaches surround it. The church there was without a pastor and a few fellow students and I committed to take services. I loved this faithful group of people. We both enjoyed getting out of the city and exploring the Gippsland countryside. On this particular day, we had been invited back to a house for Sunday dinner and I was asked, "Where do you come from, Kay?" I normally would answer, "Queensland" or occasionally, "Brisbane". However, for some reason I found myself saying, "Woodridge", without even thinking about it. The questioner's face lit up when she said," My daughter lives in Woodridge. She can't find a church to go to." Well that was amazing. Who in Victoria has ever heard of Woodridge, let alone have a relative actually living there? I pondered why I had said Woodridge in the first place without even thinking about my response.

The next Sunday I returned to the Bacchus Marsh Baptist Church where I was completing an internship. Again we had been invited back to a member's home for Sunday dinner. A young married lady asked me the same question, "Where do you come from, Kay?" "Woodridge," I answered without even thinking. She had a similar response. "My brother and his family live in Woodridge. They can't find a church to go to."

I get the message God. I will go to Woodridge and plant a church.

In order for this to actually happen I worked towards a thesis on how to pioneer a church in a neighbourhood, with specific reference to Woodridge. My research identified a whole suburb in which there were no churches. However, almost exactly in the centre of the suburb, high on a hill was the local primary school, Woodridge North. Strategies included commencing a local home group, visiting local homes, advertising in the local paper and letterbox drops. All of these endeavours were covered with prayer. I now had close to one hundred prayer supporters on the journey with me. Not only did people from Yarram and Bacchus Marsh pray for me and this pioneer ministry, several made the trip to Queensland to visit the Woodridge Wesleyan Methodist Church once it became a reality. They all had a vital part to play.

6
Permission to Fail

In the September of my final year at Kingsley, a now seven-year-old Dimity and I travelled by car, with three other Queenslanders, to attend our District Conference. This annual conference was again being held in Warwick. At the rise of conference, my name was read out as being appointed as assistant pastor to two churches, Kuraby and Western Suburbs. I was to assist the senior pastor who ministered at these two churches that were separated by a thirty-minute drive. The conference also recognised God's call to plant a church in Woodridge and stated that at some future time I would be able to work to that end.

On return to college I was at first, elated. Elated to be recognised, appointed and taken seriously. However, the first shock came when, during a weekly college chapel service, we were all asked to pray for Pastor Dennis who had just been appointed to Kuraby Church as their pastor. How can this be? Where did that leave me? There had been no communication from anyone. I didn't inquire as to what had happened but just got on with my research and the writing of my thesis.

I was studying 'Advanced Greek' at the time. My lecturer, Lyn, and I would start our classes with a walk around the block accompanied by her beloved dog, Benji, before going back to my flat for one-on-one intensive Greek. On one of these walks I expressed my apprehension about the reality of being able to start a church.

Lyn said to me, "If you go to Woodridge and it all falls apart, will that be the worst thing that has ever happened in your life?"

"No."

I had been given permission to fail.

However, it was at the conclusion of my thesis that real panic set in. It was one thing to research, theorise and plan, but how could I, an inexperienced, single mother, with very little church experience, realistically go and start a church from scratch in Woodridge? I thought: How can I get out of this? The thought came to me that if I was to get married, no one would say, "But Kay, what about Woodridge?" Instead the response more likely would have been, "Isn't it lovely that Kay has found someone and is getting married?" I did not share these private thoughts with anyone.

It was the day after this thinking that a man I had known for three years and had never looked at in a romantic light asked me out on a date. I was still thinking he was only being friendly until we got home and his romantic intentions became very clear. I preferred him as a friend and thought that the whole incident was peculiar and out of character. Within forty-eight hours, a man I hardly knew but who was loosely connected to the Bible College asked me out on a date. I enjoyed his company and we went out on a second date and then a third. It was on the fourth date that he asked me to marry him. I believed that God was clearly saying to me, "If you want to get married you can. Now choose. Marriage or ministry." I knew I had to be fully committed and focused on one or the other. It was not difficult to choose ministry. I have never regretted that choice. God knows our deepest thoughts and fears and he never forces us to follow him. When we do make that choice, it has to be for his will and purposes alone. I have seen marriage and ministry work beautifully together, however that was not the path chosen for me.

I gathered that I would now be assistant pastor in one church and not two, even though I still had heard nothing about what happened with Kuraby. I returned to Queensland in early December 1990, straight after graduation, and in time for my younger brother's twenty-first birthday celebrations. Ross had been born after I had completed my final year at high school and after my mother had suffered two miscarriages. At seventeen years of age it was such a delight to have a baby brother. He had now graduated from university and was ready to embark on his life's adventures.

The senior pastor under whom I would be working was taking holidays in December and had asked me to take three services at the Western Suburbs Church, including the one on Christmas Day. The congregation welcomed me and I felt right at home. I looked forward to returning as their assistant pastor on the third weekend in January and took a well-earned rest after the Christmas Day service.

On the day of the official commencement of my ministry, Dimity and I sat in the back row of the church. My expectation was that at some time during the service there would be an official induction of me as the assistant pastor. It never came. Instead, at the conclusion of the service the senior pastor said, "And Kay Fulcher is sitting up the back and she will be around the ridges helping people." I thought that was a strange induction, but what would I know?

The senior pastor had arranged to meet with me weekly and we had already established that I would preach once a month. I needed a month to prepare a message. So I took out my diary at that first meeting and asked: When will I be preaching again? This unexpected answer came, "You won't be preaching and you won't be leading worship. You will be able to tell a children's story, but in reality, it would be better if you went to Kuraby."

This was the first time Kuraby had been mentioned and I asked what had happened. "They didn't want a woman as their pastor. But you could go there as a member of the congregation."

So now I was being told that I was not wanted at Western Suburbs either. Even though I had already taken three services there and been warmly welcomed. It seemed strange to me that now I was being told that I could not preach after he had previously asked me to take those services while he was on holidays. When I questioned him the reply was, "There is a family that would leave the church if you preach."

My initial thinking was: Can't they just stay away one Sunday a month? I obviously did not understand the full picture. My female lecturer in Greek was an ordained minister and assistant pastor of a church in Melbourne. Beryl Baker was a year ahead of me at Kingsley College and now was pastoring a church and was due to be ordained at the Southern District Conference. I had preached in several churches in this district. To my knowledge, no objections were ever raised. I was totally bewildered.

I drove home in such a daze that I ran into the side support of the carport. I felt as if my right arm had been amputated. God had called me to preach and now I was being prevented from doing so. When the news of this spread, to my surprise I had church leaders asking me, "What are you going to do now, go back to teaching?"

That was not even a thought in my mind. God had given me a specific call and I would obey that call. I set about putting my thesis into practice. As painful as those experiences were, I am so grateful that I was not fully engaged in being an assistant pastor in two churches. That would have been a distraction from God's purposes for me in Woodridge.

Having been given an appointment by the District to serve in two churches, and having been prevented from taking up these appointments, I was left with no alternative but to start a church in Woodridge. When I say that, there is never any doubt that it was God who planted the church and that He allowed me to be in a position of having nothing else to do but obey His calling.

7
God Grows His Church

There was an entire suburb, Woodridge North, in which there were no churches. Dimity and I went to live there and Dimity went to Woodridge North Primary School to begin Year Three. I became involved in the local community, specifically my neighbourhood. This included attending school meetings; chairing a committee to establish a Neighbourhood Centre; taking cross-country training before school and the one thing I never saw myself doing, volunteering at tuckshop.[4] I met many amazing people through these activities.

I also started a nightly Bible study group in my home. This group became the basis of our church plant. My monthly prayer letters continued and faithful friends supported me in prayer. I would never underestimate the value of my supporters, mainly from Victoria. I was a new Christian when I went to Kingsley College and at that time I was, relatively, unknown amongst the Wesleyan Methodist churches in Queensland. It is totally understandable that an unknown single mother with a vision to plant a church in a place no one wanted to go, would not be taken seriously. However, I was able to be totally honest with my prayer partners in regards to my emotions, my struggles, challenges and victories. It was their belief and encouragement that enabled me to continue.

After our small group had been meeting for about six months, we decided to start Sunday services. The first hurdle was securing a venue. I asked my supporters to pray as I met with the principal of Woodridge North School. Most schools were reluctant to have churches meet on their premises but the decision was entirely up to the principal. This principal enthusiastically agreed to allow us to meet in the parents' centre and also to give us a second room for Sunday school.

I walked around the suburb and letterbox dropped a thousand leaflets and also placed an advertisement in the local paper. There were visits to nearby churches to ask for their prayer support. From these visits we had a musician, Glenda, commit to come and play for us, a young man, Peter, come and offer to start a ministry for young people, and an elderly couple, George and Jean, promised to just come. They simply loved everyone. There were others who were settled in their own churches but also committed to come and support Woodridge in the afternoons. These included John, who was a natural at welcoming people, my mother, Audrey and her friend Colleen, who were both local long-term Woodridge residents. Two young adults, and Layne and Sharon whose family I had known from that first visit to church with Kerrie and Keith, also decided to join. It was Layne who had given his testimony at that youth service where they sang 'It Came Upon the Midnight Clear.' Now adults, they decided to come to the Woodridge Church. It was delightful to see how they related so well to both those older than them and younger than them.

The first service of the Woodridge Wesleyan Methodist Church was held on July 7, 1991. Because this was an afternoon service, there were supporters from other Wesleyan Churches. However, there were also over twenty local people who came in response to one of the advertising endeavours. It seems that God had handpicked those people who He wanted to be a part of the Woodridge church. These are some stories of those people. I haven't always used their real names

On that first Sunday afternoon, I did not realise that George was standing out the front of the school. An Aboriginal family was walking by and George said, "We are having church in here this afternoon. Would you like to come and join us?"

Raymond, Debbie, Anna and Matthew came in and they too stayed. Debbie later told me that they had only decided that very morning, to leave their church and that they were walking to visit their friend, Linda, and share with her their hurt and disillusionment. They were wondering where they would now worship when George invited them in. Not only did they find a church home, but their friend Linda and her children also joined us from week two. These two families added greatly to our church family because they were always giving and loving. Linda had an amazing gift for hospitality. She lived around the corner from the church. Her home was always open and welcoming. We would often gather to just sit on the floor and sing and share stories and whatever food we had. This fellowship was certainly something very special.

Alf and Dulcie were a very endearing elderly Christian couple. They were content in their church. When they received the letterbox leaflet, they promptly threw it in the bin and didn't give it another thought. Two nights later, Alf woke in the middle of the night with a strong prompting to go and get that leaflet from the bin. They prayed and both felt that God was telling them to come. What a delightful addition they were to our church family. They loved unconditionally, they accepted without question or judgment and they constantly gave from their garden and possessions. Everyone learned so much from them. They demonstrated Christ. I am sure God chose them to be foundational members of the Woodridge Wesleyan Methodist Church to bless everyone who, He knew, would come and join us.

Keith and Joy were another local retired couple who loved the Lord. They too had no thought of leaving their church but when they saw the advertisement in the local paper, they were drawn to the map of Australia with the flame in the centre. This was the symbol of the Australian Wesleyan Methodist Church at that time. They also attended the first service and stayed, becoming incredible influencers. Their son had married Margaret's daughter. Margaret moved into the same retirement village and also came to our baby church.

Margaret was one of a kind. The joy of the Lord was her strength. Margaret chose to walk to the local shops and services rather than drive. In this way she could meet people who were in their gardens or were just passing by her. She had a gift for meeting people who were in crisis and loving them. This included a family of five who had been evicted from their home. Margaret met them when all of their belongings had been thrown out onto the footpath. The church family gathered together and help re-house the family. Margaret brought the three children to Sunday school for several years and they became such loved members of our church family. Margaret was so faithful in her commitment to love that she touched many lives. Not the least, that of her nephew, Hugh.

Hugh was the son of Margaret's brother. His mother died when he was a small boy. He had come home from school and found his mother unresponsive in her bedroom. Hugh was so scared that he hid under his bed until his father came home from work. It seemed like neither of them fully recovered. Hugh missed out on the love and nurture of a mother and was riddled with guilt for hiding and not knowing what to do for his mother.

In his early teens, Hugh turned to substance abuse, beginning with sniffing glue or petrol. He progressed to other drugs and his life was in jeopardy by the time he reached twenty. Hugh spent years in and out of drug rehab centres until finally receiving some healing for his drug addiction through a Salvation Army rehabilitation centre. He was still a heavy smoker and consumed alcohol, however, he was free from other drugs.

Margaret never gave up on Hugh and was a constant source of love in his life. She brought Hugh to church and we were given the privilege of loving him also. He was unable to hold down paid work but he contributed mightily to our church family. I would come home from a day of visiting, to find Hugh mowing my lawn. He turned up one day with a lounge suite in a trailer because he knew I only had two beanbag chairs. He was a living example of how anyone in the church who had a need, received exactly what was required from someone else in the church, without asking for it.

Another person God arranged to be a part of our church was Ray. Ray was originally from New Zealand, he had a Methodist background and he taught at the Woodridge Primary School. He had previously been travelling twenty-five kilometres away to attend a Wesleyan Methodist Church in Fortitude Valley. This was not easy as he did not have a car and the journey involved catching two trains and lots of walking.

He, too, saw the advertisement in the local paper and came to our first service. Ray also had a gift for hospitality. He loved to put on hangis[5] in his backyard. Everyone enjoyed this traditional Maori style of cooking. He would invite the whole church family but would also invite neighbours and people he had met on his travels. It was a very multi-cultural gathering. These were amazing times of fellowship, singing and food. We had a wedding in his backyard and also dedication services for babies and children. Some of these people seeking God were not yet attending church services. However, church is much more than Sunday services. The fellowship of these gatherings drew people to more formal attendances. More than one of the men I met at Ray's gatherings told me they had broken every one of the Ten Commandments and that they did not belong in church. How marvellous then, when one such man walked into a church, removed his hat and fitted in with the congregation. It is amazing how powerful love and acceptance can prove to be. Ray was certainly a point of connection for many people.

Joan had an adult daughter, Joanne, who was severely disabled. Joanne was non-verbal but would make noises from time to time. The elders at Joan's previous church had told her that Joanne's noises interrupted the work of the Holy Spirit. Joan was so hurt that she decided to leave. She was looking for somewhere else to go where Joanne would not be seen as a disruption. We loved them both. Joanne expressed delight in our simple worship and we delighted in her.

The beginning of the next school year saw a change of principal at the school. This could have been a problem as not too many principals were inclined towards allowing churches to meet in their schools. The church family and my prayer team prayed. The new principal was a man called Chris Plant. I had gone to high school with Chris. We also went to Teachers College together and our friendship had grown there. Neither of us were Christians at the time. When we met again, we both had faith journeys to share. Chris had married a pastor's daughter. He responded positively to the request for the church to continue to meet at his school. God knows every detail and His work and timing is amazing.

The Woodridge Wesleyan Methodist Church received such favour and support and we always felt welcome in the school community. I remember one Christmas Day, a teacher drove from her home to the church to drop off a gift and thank the church for their influence on the school. Another teacher, who was part of a different church, brought a student and his mother to our church. She was concerned about David and his behaviour and was prompted to invite his mother to church. She could have taken them to her own church but, because this church was in their own neighbourhood, she brought them to us.

The following week the whole family joined. Claire, Roger and their five boys were instantly loved and welcomed. We journeyed together through many crises. Claire had grown up in foster care and Margaret became a surrogate mother to Claire and grandmother to her five boys. It was a beautiful family though not without its struggles. As Claire became involved in a home group and established relationships with God, as well as with the other ladies, her life began to change.

Some of her friends resented the changes and the fact that Claire was no longer joining them in some of their questionable activities. As I visited Claire one day, there were two women on the footpath ready to confront me. They told me that they had come to "bash me up" for taking Claire away from them. I knew Claire, along with her youngest son, was watching. My natural instinct, from childhood, was to fight back, plan my defensive moves and counterattack. However, I knew that I could not do that. No ducking and weaving. I just had to stand there and take a beating. I dropped what I had in my hands, put my arms by my side and said: Okay, come and hit me. They approached me but then stopped and walked away. I'm glad that Claire and her son did not have to witness a beating.

Ros walked up the hill to church and John made her feel so welcome that she not only stayed but also became leader of our children's ministry. Linda had just moved into the area with her daughter, leaving behind an abusive relationship. She too, lived on a street within walking distance of the church.

Paul, Debbie and their three girls, Laura, Leisel and Heather lived in the street leading up to the school where we held our church services. As a family, they always went to church on Christmas Day. However, on this Christmas Day, in that first year of our church, they dressed and got in their car ready to go. The car didn't start. They remembered getting a calendar and leaflet about a church being held at the school, so they walked up and came to the Christmas Day service. They expected this to be a one-off visit. However, not only did they stay, but each became a significant Christian leader. Paul preached his first sermon with us and Debbie became a Sunday school teacher. Heather was only a few months old when they first attended and she grew up in our church. I will always remember our first church camp when she was nearly two and George was in his eighties. We drew partners to serve during the weekend, including guiding them through sensory adventures, taking care of their practical needs and also washing each other's feet on Good Friday. George drew Heather. She so lovingly washed his feet and guided him all through Easter. It was a powerful image of love, service and humility and captured the attitude of the whole family.

The second Christmas Day saw two more local neighbourhood families come to church. Alma lived next door to the church and Carola lived across the road. These two ladies and their families became treasured friends and grew together in their love of, and commitment to, Jesus. I recently saw Carola at Alma's funeral and we both reflected on those five-shared years in the Woodridge church as being very significant and special.

Soon I knew everyone in every house surrounding the church. They were friends and neighbours. Irene and her three girls came to church. Carola's friend, Vicky, and her girls came to church. Dimity was safe to ride and skate around the streets and brought her friends to church also. This is how our congregation grew and was strengthened by word of mouth.

One exception was the three boys who found themselves in church by default. During a service, we could hear children playing in the trees outside our building and being quite noisy. George went outside and we all knew that he would be gentle with them when he asked them to be quiet. Five minutes later, George came back inside with the three boys he found. They stayed for the remainder of the service and went out for Sunday school. I have no idea what George said to them, but I went home with them to explain where they had been. They lived with their grandmother across the road from the school. Their father was in prison and no one knew where their mother was. Next week they turned up for church again, washed, groomed and in their best clothes. They left when their father was released but while they were with us they brought us great joy.

God kept bringing people to the church. Some stayed a short time, people such as Maureen, Kelli Ann, Ty and little Ben. Ben had advanced abdominal cancer and the family had moved down from Toowoomba for his treatment. Toowoomba is a city one and a half hours drive from Brisbane. Though they had good hospitals there, the best children's oncology facilities were in Brisbane. The Woodridge area provided cheap accommodation. We treasured the time we had with this family. Ben was such a beautiful boy. The family left no stone unturned in caring for him. However, he was only three when he died. "Jesus, Mummy. Jesus" were the last words Ben said. The impact was profound on all of us.

The end of our second year saw another change of principal. Chris Plant had only been a temporary appointee. Now Woodridge North was to receive their permanent principal. We again faced uncertainty. I went to meet the new principal and ask permission to continue to use the two rooms on a Sunday. I saw a familiar face. Brian Clark had been the deputy principal in my first year of teaching at Woodridge Primary School. He was the one who had brought Hayden's father to my classroom to thank me.

Now, twenty years later, here is Brian, the principal from whom I am seeking favour. Brian surprised me by saying that he did not think we could have those rooms any more, but he quickly went on to say that they were not good enough. The school numbers had declined. There was a whole wing that was not being used. He continued by saying, "It is a permanent building, not a temporary one like you have been using. No one else will be using it, so you can set it up however you like and leave it like that all the time."

This was beyond my wildest expectations. The excitement amongst the church family was palpable. We had working bees to which every single person came, and such fun was had, as we painted, carpeted, and decorated the two rooms. One was for the worship services and the other was for the children's ministry. Jean donated her piano. Alf was a skilled wood worker and made a lectern and beautiful communion trays. Gifted sewers made banners. There was so much joy. We planned a celebration for our first service followed by a lunch in the lovely courtyard downstairs.

Wendy was a friend of Debbie's and I knew her mainly because her son was in Dimity's class, but I had also worked with her in the school tuckshop where she made me feel welcome. Because of our connection, I invited her and her family to come to our special service. Wendy said she would love to come but that her husband would never agree. She told me the story. How when her husband, Graham, was a young boy, his mother was quite sick, and his father sent him and his brother to Sunday school mainly to give her some peace and quiet. It was December school holidays and there was a nativity scene set up in a sandbox. Graham and his brother delighted in playing war games in the sand pit with the figurines. They were both asked to go home and never return. Graham had felt negative towards church ever since, and Wendy knew that he would never come.

However, God knew differently. Graham was a salesman who regularly travelled to North Queensland and was away at this very time. He usually stayed with friends on his trips and always enjoyed the company of others. At one location however, his friends had other visitors and unfortunately Graham had to spend a night in a motel room by himself. He struggled with loneliness and boredom so resorted to reading the Gideon Bible in the bedside drawer. God spoke to him as he read and when he arrived home, he suggested to Wendy that they should go to church as a family. Wendy was able to say, "Well, as a matter of fact, we have been invited to go to church on Sunday." Another delightful family joined with us and again we grew together around God's Word.

God had laid a platform of like-minded Christians to make this church a reality. He then set about building His church. My mother was a significant participant in the birth of this church. When I invited Mum to come to my baptism, her response was, "Wasn't what your father and I did for you as a baby good enough?" I couldn't answer but she did reluctantly come. She continued to come and to bring her friend Colleen. Her attendance did not wane when I went to Bible College. In fact she became more involved and was not just seen as Kay's mother.

Even before we started church services, I took Colleen through 'Christianity Explained'. Colleen only agreed to do the course if Audrey would do it with her. When we got to the question, "Why should God let you into Heaven?" Mum's answers reflected her godly life and that she truly was a good woman. After an explanation about the free gift of grace, it was like a light bulb came on for Mum. In so many ways we were opposites, including our God-given gifts and abilities. I knew full well of my many shortcomings but had experienced God's grace, forgiveness and love. In contrast, my mother had hardly put a foot wrong her whole life believing in the value of being a good person. Her response to this awakening was, "Is that all there is to it?" She glowed in her newfound understanding. While I had envisaged Colleen coming to faith through this study, it was my own mother who taught me not to take faith and understanding for granted. Mum was brilliant at administration and was a rock for me and for many others.

Not everybody slotted in beautifully to church life. I met Sally through the ministry of Fusion. The contact I had with the Fusion Movement was through the family I met at Bacchus Marsh years earlier who had a sister who lived in Woodridge. They ran life skills classes for local Woodridge women. Sally was a young single mother with a four-year-old daughter. It was a challenge to visit her home. It was never clean or tidy and it was difficult to put one foot in front of the other without stepping on something. There were plates with unfinished food and obvious signs of vermin. However, this did not dissuade me from visiting her.

We started doing 'Christianity Explained' together and she seemed very open to God being in her life. Sally had a much older boyfriend but he broke up with her, stating that he could no longer live in that environment. She was so devastated and tried everything to get him to take her back. When he didn't budge, she took matters into her own hands. Sally placed a personal advertisement in the paper and set about sleeping with as many men as she could. Her aim was to get pregnant as quickly as she could, tell her ex-boyfriend that the baby was his, and then surely, he would come back. I couldn't believe that she was actually telling me this plan. She did get pregnant and her boyfriend did come back. However, she suffered a miscarriage soon after. Once I had supported her through her stay in hospital, my mind was made up that I would not support her any longer. She had crossed the bounds of what I considered reasonable. There were other people who I could spend time with. That's when God spoke to me with a very clear question.

"What makes you think that I can't do the same thing in Sally's life that I did in yours?"

I was instantly rebuked and convicted. I was again challenged about prejudices that I did not think I had. God's love has no limits. My visits continued but soon afterwards Sally and her boyfriend moved away from the area. I introduced them to a pastor in their new suburb. He did 'Christianity Explained' with both of them. They both committed their lives to Jesus. The transformation was amazing to me, but not to God.

8
Battlegrounds

The church continued to grow. We still had afternoon services, with some people attending their home church in the morning and supporting us in the afternoon. The local people, most of whom lived within walking distance of the church, wanted to move to morning services. We expected that we would lose some people with this move, however, those who had been attending two churches all decided to continue with Woodridge. Each one was a treasured blessing. On the surface it appeared like one glorious ride with God at the helm.

However, it was not an easy ride. Living by faith was a great learning curve that also brought about many blessings. Similarly, as a church we were never concerned about what we didn't have. Our church family shared our lives and our possessions and became lifelong friends.

Although I knew it was God's plan for me to put all my energy into Woodridge, I was also very much aware that the main reason that the district church leaders allowed me to do this was that they did not know what else to do with me. I didn't know it at the time, but later found out, that there was an expectation of failure amongst the church leaders. The church did not meet the "normal" hallmarks of a church in regard to buildings, resources and finances. The fact that others did not take this church seriously should not have mattered to me, however I did feel lonely and unsupported. In contrast there was tremendous support and encouragement from my prayer team, many of whom had travelled from Victoria to visit.

Before the first service in Woodridge, I visited other Wesleyan Methodist Churches to share about the new church commencing, I had a young university student named Peter approach me. He said that he would like to be a part of what we were doing in Woodridge. He had a passion for youth, especially those young people who had no knowledge of God or any experience of church. He wanted to come to Woodridge, meet young people in the parks or on the streets and build relationships with them. Peter proved to be gifted at doing this very thing.

Teenage boys and young men especially trusted him and gravitated towards him. I approached the Woodridge Police Citizens Youth Club to see if we could use their facilities. They were only too happy to hear that someone was positively working with the youth of Woodridge. They offered us their facilities for free on a Saturday night. This was beyond our expectations. They had great facilities, including a fully equipped gymnasium, basketball court, volleyball court and a well-equipped kitchen. Peter gathered the young people together and they all attended the Saturday night activities. John and Shirley Antonio, an older couple with a lot of experience in the field of youth work, came to support Peter and to provide food for all who came. These were exciting nights and there was never a concern with behaviour or poor discipline. We all grew to love and appreciate these young people.

One Saturday night, Peter arrived straight from his

part-time job. He left his bag, containing his wages, in the kitchen. After everyone had gone and he went to lock-up he discovered that all of his cash was missing. He was distraught. He told me that he did not want to continue. He had come to help these people and they had taken advantage of him. He was hurt and disillusioned. John, Shirley and I attempted to continue the ministry. However, Peter was the glue that held it together and he was the one who had built the relationships. It was hard to see Peter leave. We all loved him and valued his place in our church. I felt that I had let him down in not knowing how to comfort and encourage him.

Rather than see the end of this program, I asked the youth leader from the local Church of Christ if he would be willing to take it over. I had met Luke on several occasions. He lived in the area and had a heart for the local youth. He and his church were only too happy to take over Saturday nights at the Police-Citizens Youth Club.

It was a great joy to hear that, just a few months later, some of those young men had turned their lives around. Luke and his church conducted their baptisms and welcomed them into their church family with great love and celebration. Some plant and others water, but it is God who causes the growth.

There were more challenges to come. It was a year later when Dimity and I were watching television on a Sunday night that our relaxing evening was rudely interrupted. It was rainy and windy but the noise I heard coming from my bedroom immediately made me think: that sounds like someone coming through the venetian blinds. I walked down the hallway towards the bedroom and halfway down, hearing the wind and rain, I relaxed, thinking it was just the weather. As I turned to go into my bedroom to close the window, I was suddenly face-to-face with a large man dressed in black and wearing a balaclava. Without thinking I screamed, "Get out of here you mongrel!" He climbed back out of the window through the blinds, and I climbed out after him, chasing him down the street, screaming as I went. Because of the wind and rain, no one heard me except Dimity who had come into the bedroom and found it empty. Panic set in for her. Thankfully my pursuit was in vain, because catching up with him surely would have ended badly.

I returned home to comfort Dimity, ring the police, the owner of the house and my brother, Ross. Police happened to be nearby with sniffer dogs. They picked up the trace of drugs, but no intruder. My empty handbag was found the next day in a neighbour's yard.

This incident made us realise how vulnerable we were living in a lowset house. The owner was only too happy to put security screens on all the windows and doors, which went a long way to relieving our anxiety.

A second break-in happened a year later. I was away for a week at a pastor's retreat. Everyone in the neighbourhood knew that I was away for the week and that Dimity had gone to stay with my mother. When the retreat finished, I went to our house to change before picking up Dimity. The first thing noticeable when I walked through the front door was the TV and VCR were both gone. That didn't worry me. My thinking was that Mum had come to get them to help fill her time with Dimity. What did worry me was when I walked into the kitchen and saw the griller tray pulled out, toast crumbs everywhere on the benches and floor, the butter and Vegemite out of the fridge and dirty dishes in the sink. I then walked around the house and found towels draped over all of the windows. That is when the penny dropped. Someone had been living in my house.

It had to be someone who knew the house was empty. They took their time to go through every nook and cranny and steal anything of any value. They then packed the goods into my own suitcases and absconded. We didn't want to live there anymore.

It was a busy life, being a mother, studying for my Master's degree in biblical languages and pastoring the church with an essential emphasis on pastoral care. One specific time when I felt particularly burdened, I initiated a conversation with my then now ten-year-old daughter where I revealed to her that I felt I could not continue in the ministry. I will never forget her response. "You didn't drag me to Melbourne for three years to be teased by boys to give up on being a pastor." God's call was on my life, but Dimity came along for the ride. She was not just a passenger. She was a vital part of every process and would often encourage, rebuke and challenge me. We continued onwards.

Thankfully, we were able to move into a highset house with a secure fence and gate. It had a big back yard and was ideally suitable for the ministries we started there. They included a playgroup run by Carola, a library organised by my mother, Audrey, and a youth group, that I headed up myself. We had between twenty and thirty local youth attend every Friday night. Apart from Dimity, Carmen, Laura, Leisel and David, no one else was a part of the church. We set up a computer downstairs along with gym equipment, and a basketball hoop in the backyard. It was a safe place for youth to drop in at any time.

At the end of our first year of youth ministry, we planned a weekend camp away at the Tallebudgera National Fitness campsite. This is a wonderful campsite on Queensland's Gold Coast. The facilities and the location are first class. We had twenty-eight local young people attend. What a fantastic weekend! Everyone was so well behaved and asking to help in any way they could. We ran our own church service on the Sunday morning and for the majority of the teenagers this was their first such experience. Everybody left that camp on an absolute high.

It was strange to see my mother standing at the top of the verandah when we arrived home. I thought something must be wrong, and sure enough there was. Again, it was obvious to everyone in the neighbourhood that the house was empty for the weekend because we had met there on Friday afternoon to pack cars and organise transport. Someone had used a glasscutter to get in the fixed glass door at the top of the back verandah. The police concluded that it had to be a small child to get through that space and that they were wearing socks on their hands. From there, the front door was opened, and the thieves took everything we had replaced from the previous break-in, plus my computer, laser printer and even the discs containing my Masters thesis.

Dimity and I were both devastated. We thought we were now living in a safe house, but we were wrong. The thing that hurt me most of all was not the lost possessions, nor the thought of thieves being in our house going through our belongings, it was the knowledge that this was probably someone in the neighbourhood. Someone who knew we were away must have also been aware of what we were doing from our house to assist those in the neighbourhood. I guess I felt the same as Peter did years previously: I've come here to help people, and this is how I have been treated.

I went to bed but instead of sleeping, began to plan how I could make the premises even safer. In my mind, this included installing rolls of barbed wire and putting broken glass on the roof. I realised how silly this was. In my head I knew God was our protector and in none of the break-ins had either of us been injured. However, in the front of my mind, I was depressed and could not get out of bed. I would get up for breakfast and to get Dimity off to school and then go back to bed. I did that for three days, not communicating with anyone. People must have been praying for me because on the third day there was a complete breakthrough.

I got out of bed determined to continue.

This was not of my own strength. I remember looking out at the roof where I had planned to put barbed wire and broken glass and I said: No! I am not leaving. God has called me here. I drive in a stake proclaiming this neighbourhood for Jesus and I will not be driven out! Victory was complete. There was not a backward step to be taken.

Church life flourished as we grew together. Whenever there was an event at the school, people would ask what our building was. Everyone knew, "Oh, that's the church." No one seemed to think that it was strange having a church in the school grounds. However, someone was obviously not happy. Dimity and I had just left to go on a camping holiday at the end of our fourth year in Woodridge, when, on the first day of the holiday, I got a message that there had been a fire at the school. In fact, our entire building had been burnt to the ground. Nothing else in the school had been touched. We drove back to assess the damage. The only things I was able to salvage from the wreckage were two semi-burnt pages from a hymnbook. Everything else was totally destroyed.

When Brian Clark told his wife that the church had been burnt down, she responded by saying that it hadn't. The church is the people. She was right. The people were amazing. I was dwelling on all that we had lost. I thought about all the hard work they had put into that building and of all the contributions made to make it so special. However their responses taught me lesson in positivity. They were excited to be going back to our *old* building where we had such good memories. That's where it all began.

It was towards the end of my fifth year in Woodridge that God spoke to me about moving on. I was aware that so often I did not know what I was doing and that the people needed someone with more experience to take them onwards. It was when reading aloud the passage where God took Moses up on the mountain to see the Promised Land and told him that he would not go there, that God spoke to me. You are not the one to take the people on. Although tears rolled down my face, I knew that it was the right time for me to move on and the best time for the church. I was though, praying for just the right person to be their next pastor.

I kept thinking of Rex and Lien. Rex was ahead of me in Bible College and I knew how much he loved God. Rex and Lien both had amazing testimonies and I believed that the people would love and accept them. Rex had been pastoring in Victoria and I understood he had wisdom and experience to offer. After prayer one morning I rang. Lien answered but said that Rex was still in bed. I joked about that when he came to the phone, as it was then past nine o'clock. He replied that he hadn't slept because he had been up all night praying. He believed it was time for him to move from his church and he was asking God to show him where to go. I said that I had rung to ask if he would consider a call to Woodridge. He said he would.

I was so excited. I believed that God had organised the right people to take over the church, live in the area and become a part of the community. I passed on the story to my District Superintendent and asked him to follow up with Rex.

Some time passed and I heard that someone else was being appointed to Woodridge. Being curious as to what had happened with Rex, I asked my superintendent what Rex had said.

His reply was, "We didn't contact him. We wanted someone who could continue unsalaried."

I was dumbfounded, but realistically God still worked. Rex accepted a call to pastor a church in Rockhampton and the Woodridge Church was placed in good hands.

As I was about to leave Woodridge, the senior pastor to whom I had been initially appointed as an assistant asked me, "How are you going to feel when you leave Woodridge and the whole thing falls apart?"

I replied, "God didn't plant the church in Woodridge to have it all fall apart." And it did not.

9
My Dream Job

The call to Woodridge had been so clear and specific that I didn't seek ministry elsewhere when I left. God had called me to do something and had then showed me when it was time to move on. My ministry was over, so I went back to teaching. A position was advertised at Calvary College, a Christian school with two campuses in different suburbs of Logan City.

Logan City is divided almost in half by the Pacific Highway. Those suburbs on the western side of the highway were considered the less desirable and of a perceived lower socio-economic standard. Woodridge was on the west. The Christian campuses were on the east. The position was for their first ever primary school physical education teacher.

The job entailed planning curriculum and teaching in both campuses that were twenty minutes apart. As the college had not previously employed a specialist physical education teacher, I had the absolute thrill of setting everything in motion, including the writing of the curriculum and the purchasing of equipment. The children were fantastic and really embraced the program. It was the best job I had ever had.

The original campus of the college was a very special place. I was not the only one who testified to feeling the presence of God on the property. The staff would meet for devotions and prayer every morning, where, if anyone had a particular need, that prayer took precedence over everything else. There was a real sense of joy and of faith amongst the staff.

Dimity and I returned to the church which we had first attended with Kerrie and Keith ten years ago. They had a great youth group where the leaders emphasised discipleship. Dimity made good friends and grew in her faith. When she turned fourteen it was wonderful to see her being baptised and to observe others sowing into her life. I was happy to not be involved in any particular ministry. However, about once every six months, I was asked to preach at the evening service. I loved those opportunities to share God's Word with the evening congregation.

Towards the end of my second year at Calvary, I was sharing the morning devotion. I remember reading from Revelation and tears started to run down my face. It wasn't that the passage was especially poignant but rather that God was speaking to me.

"This is what you are supposed to be doing with your life: sharing God's Word."

As everyone went to their classrooms, I went and sat by the pond to pray. Dawn, a Year One teacher, came and put her hand on my shoulder. "Kay," she said, "God has just told me that you will go out with joy and share the Gospel."

I pondered the events of the morning as I went about that day. That evening, a member of a leadership team from a large church, in another city, contacted me to ask if I would consider coming on staff as an assistant pastor.

Because of the morning's events I certainly considered the invitation seriously.

Prayerful consideration soon saw the appropriate end of my dream job and a return to a pastoral role. This position was markedly different from my experiences at Woodridge. When I went to Woodridge, the only clear knowledge I had was of God's call to go. He planted the church, one by one. I cared for the flock, but I also felt the loneliness of ministry. This was a large, multi-staffed church that was well resourced and extremely well organised. There were three on the pastoral team, as well as a music director, office manager and other part-time employees. I had specific roles and was now to receive a salary for the first time in formal ministry. I had high expectations of this experience of ministry.

Many of these expectations were met as the church continued to grow, and I loved fulfilling my roles. To an outside observer, I'm sure the church presented as a flourishing success. Closer observations caused me to realise that not everything was healthy. As new people continued to come, many also left, often without explanation.

During my second year, it seemed everything I did was criticised and undermined. This criticism was not related to my ministry, but about my character. There was the potential for trust to be eroded. I was confused and emotionally affected to the point of having panic attacks. After several months of struggling, I went to see a Christian counsellor. The counsellor helped me see that my loyalty was always to be primarily to God. She was also able to remind me of the spiritual resources at my disposal and hold me accountable for my own spiritual health.

It wasn't until I read an article in the newspaper entitled, 'Toxic Bosses'- that I understood what was happening. The article described exactly the scenario I faced in the workplace, which boiled down to:

1. A boss for whom the most important factor was an unquestioning loyalty to him or her.

2. Playing favourites with staff members and setting others against a particular person.

3. Spreading untruths and generating an atmosphere of distrust of anyone except for the boss.

4. Overextending financial resources so that the budget was never quite met, thereby, always creating a need for more contributions.

5. A lack of accountability in regard to finances.

This article helped me realise that the situation I was in was an identifiable scenario and that it was not uncommon. I have since heard of many stories from people with similar experiences in their workplace. In all cases, leaving proved to be the best option.

I wanted to leave but my daughter was thriving in this church. When I mentioned to her that I wanted to go, she declared that she was not leaving. I would not leave her there on her own. I got up earlier than usual to pray and ask God what to do. I opened the Bible at my bookmark and the first verse I read was, "Do not go out in haste." I therefore decided to stay until God showed me otherwise.

I needed to be faithful to God, respect the leadership and minister to hurting people. I was now being openly criticised from the pulpit and at no time did I feel that it was appropriate to defend myself. I again went on my knees to God. My prayer was: God, I cannot stay in my own strength. If you want me to stay, please give me the wisdom and strength that I need. It was then that I believe God spoke to me and said, "Go out with dignity."

Now my first task was to tell Dimity that, for me, leaving was not optional. My emotional health was deteriorating, and I had to get out of the situation. Only a few months had passed since her stated determination to stay and yet, now her response was, "Where will we go Mum?" Now that Dimity was sixteen, I knew that God was opening her eyes and her understanding so that there would be no division between us.

We moved on together to the place God had prepared for us. Dimity thrived and made life-long friends and I healed. I am so thankful that God's grace and the passing of time does allow for total healing. Part of that healing required my forgiveness from the heart.

I pondered if I had made a mistake going there. Had I heard God's voice incorrectly? I don't believe so. The outcomes for me personally were not great. However, the lessons learnt, the battles fought and the loss of naive trust in the structured church, all helped equip me for future life and ministry. I was again reminded that God's call does not mean an easy road. There are always battles, challenges and struggles.

Naively, I still expected that when God called and you followed, success would be the result. Life and ministry can be a battlefield, but it is not always about winning or succeeding. Ministry should never be about personal success. I remembered my conversation with Lyn and understanding that there was always permission to fail. The Holy Spirit can take any opportunity to glorify Jesus if we surrender our feelings and expectations and merely focus on being set ablaze by our devotion to him. Circumstances are often not *fair*. It is not up to us to demand, seek or expect fairness.

The purpose of the battle is not personal victory. God's purposes are always to make us one with Him. The success or failure of individual tasks may prove to be insignificant in the light of His eternal plan. What He desires of us is availability and obedience. All of our experiences, successes and failures can be used by God to draw us closer to total abandonment and trust in Him. That knowledge makes me thankful for every hardship. "I being in the way, the Lord led me."[7]

10

The Dream Returned

The year of 2000 was significant for both Dimity and me. Dimity chose the church we would attend now that she agreed we both needed to leave. Dimity has always kept the close friends she made at this new church. Jillian and Dimity were bridesmaids for each other and have kept each other on track spiritually, in addition to sharing lots of fun and adventures. God provided above and beyond all we could have imagined.

This was also Dimity's important final year of high school. It was a real benefit for me to be available to be involved as much as was needed. I was able to be the scorer for her Premiership-winning softball team. She was able to participate in an early entry university program and to thrive in her academic program. Teaching her to drive was a great stress for both of us. On one occasion we both got out of the car and refused to drive home, abandoning the vehicle behind us. However, it was good to be present at these milestones and to see her begin to transition into adulthood. These things also helped me to heal.

Leaving our previous church with dignity was possible

because of my purposeful intent not to make disparaging remarks about anyone or anything. A flood of love encompassed me as I left. The most startling comment was written on a giant card and came from a young girl who I didn't even know and with whom I had no personal interaction. She wrote, "You influence me." Those words stayed with me, making me aware that there are observations of you and conclusions being drawn about you, when you don't even realise it.

Because of my emotional state, I had not applied for any jobs or even seriously considered how I was going to earn a living. As a forty-seven-year-old, I was even considering taking on casual work stacking supermarket shelves. I knew I needed time to recover and consider the future.

Two things happened to change my mind. Firstly, I received, in the mail, an invitation to attend Amsterdam 2000, the Billy Graham Worldwide Evangelism Conference to be held in The Netherlands in July 2000. I didn't know how it came that I was even invited. Later it was revealed that my District Superintendent, Stan Baker, had invited me. He wanted me to know that he believed in my future in ministry.

The second thing happened when I rang my previous school, Calvary Christian College, where I had been in my dream job, to organise a date to speak at chapel. I had spoken once a term at the Springwood campus since I had left, and I really enjoyed the ongoing interaction with the staff and students. The phone call was made just a few days before the start of the school year. I wanted to book an early date in case I did get a job. The registrar asked me to hold and passed me on to the principal. Not an hour before my phone call, the teacher who had replaced me, had come into the school with her husband to say they were going to be missionaries in Indonesia much sooner than expected. Her resignation left the school without a physical education teacher just days before the start of the school year. I was ringing to request an early booking for chapel because of my imminent job-hunting and here was a job presented to me. Interviews followed and I started back at my dream job with no gap in pay cheques. God's timing again proved to be impeccable.

Attending the Amsterdam 2000 Billy Graham conference was an amazing experience. It was such a blessing to sit under the ministry of so many profound teachers and preachers. I was greatly impacted by people such as Steve Saint, and Joni Erickson Tada, Anne Graham Lotz and attendees from Rwanda. Anne spoke on the first evening expecting her father to be present. He, however, could not travel due to ill health but was able to watch on video. After Ann greeted her Heavenly Father and her earthly father, she preached a very powerful message from Isaiah Chapter Six. As I sat there, my thoughts went to imagining what a great joy and blessing it must be for Billy Graham to see his daughter in this light. Of all the things he had achieved, and all the fame he knew, this had to be a shining light for him. My musings were on my own daughter and my potent desire that in whatever I did or did not do, I would raise a godly daughter?

The conference rekindled my desire for mission and to fulfil God's call to preach the gospel to the poor. In my report back to my District Conference, I reflected on the lack of intentional evangelism in our churches. Each year the majority of local church reports would present "zero" as their number of salvations. I failed to understand how this was possible. I never saw myself as an evangelist, but I also never understood how Christians could not talk about Jesus and demonstrate his love. Seeing people come to faith in Jesus did not make me an evangelist but that seemed to be the reputation I had.

One of the last items on the District Conference agenda was the stationing sheet. The name of every church is read out, together with the pastors appointed to minister there in the coming year. I was not appointed to any church, but as an ordained minister, my name should have been read out as an unstationed elder. It was not. I sat there thinking that either it was an accidental omission, or I was no longer considered worthy.

There was an announcement that there would be an extra meeting of the District Board before the rise of conference. I was advised to attend this meeting. Still not knowing what was going on, I nervously attended the meeting. It was here that I was invited to take up the role of District Evangelist. I was again faced with a decision. Should I leave the well-paid job I loved, or undertake an untested role with a dubious income, yet doing what I believe God had called me to do? It was not a difficult decision.

The fact that Dimity had decided to spend a year in the USA made it easier for me to also move on. She participated in a young adults discipleship program with Kingdom Building Ministries in Denver, Colorado and then moved on to an internship with the First Wesleyan Church in Greensborough, North Carolina. Her leaving home made it easier for me to undertake this appointment.

This was to be an itinerant ministry, travelling and spending time in several churches. I was able to work with small groups in various churches across the South Queensland district. My role was to equip and resource. One of the first things I did in preparation for my role was to travel to Sydney to train with the Evangelism Explosion organisation. Along with providing me with skills and knowledge, I met some amazing people like Langdon and Virginia. They sowed into my life and continue to be amazing role models. We have been able to share in each other's ministries for many years. I loved growing together with many Christians who were keen to be active in sharing their faith. I also found it extremely rewarding to be involved in outreach programs in local communities. In one church, I worked one day a week at their low-cost grocery ministry, listening to the stories of the customers and having the opportunity to build relationships.

Towards the end of 2001, a church that was looking for a pastor contacted me. I had not actually been working with this church but knew that they had gone through a painful church split. The chairman of the search committee rang and asked if I would consider a call to be their pastor. There was a very quick answer of "No." He reacted by asking if I would at least pray about it. I did pray. I prayed, "God please send them someone to love them." And there it was: God's voice, "You go and love them." I don't know why my instant response was a negative one. Perhaps it was because I was enjoying the varied role of District Evangelist or else it was because I was not looking for such a challenge as rebuilding a church that had been damaged. I still felt totally inadequate. One thing I learnt very early on in ministry is that it is not about what I want to do. When you present yourself to God and say that you will go anywhere, He takes you at your word. I therefore made myself available for the interview process. I loved the people and felt that together we could go on a journey towards healing and being a positive influence in the community.

Everyone had been hurt in some way and perhaps they needed someone who understood their pain so that together, we could be brought to wholeness. I didn't expect it to be easy, but nothing prepared me for the journey that lay ahead.

There was an obvious sense of ownership among some of the people who had kept the church going after the split. So much so that I was yelled at for getting out a knife to cut a birthday cake. It was not my kitchen and I needed to ask if I wanted anything. There were many incidents like this, but I was not overly concerned until our first quarterly congregation meeting. Every report was fiercely criticised. Grown men were brought to tears, and I was in a state of shock.

Every room in the main church building, except for the actual worship centre, was cluttered, mainly with junk obtained from auctions and deemed to be useful "one day." The brick building at the highest point of the property was now nothing more than a storeroom for old pews, second hand furniture and random pieces of electrical equipment. Two demountable classrooms were also on the property, but these, too, were unusable because of accumulated clutter. The board decided we needed a physical clean up to mirror the spiritual health we all desired. This saw the church pull together at working bees. Clearing out junk, painting, cleaning and gardening saw the property transformed, but again there was aggressive criticism for every undertaking. There were times when the criticism was taken on board and decisions were changed. The criticism did not stop. It seemed that anything the board decided was disputed. There were those who had decided that they would never trust a pastor again and, therefore I had to be stopped from having any control or influence whatsoever.

The board understood what was happening. The atmosphere was so negative that I would pray that no new people would come to church as the experience could well put them off Christianity.

We all loved the people who were critical and negative, and still do, but attempts to express our desire for God's love to flow within the church family, were met with disdain.

"So, you are saying all we have to do is love each other?"

"Yes," I replied, "that is to be our focus."

Their response was, "No. We all just have to work harder and give more."

The atmosphere was so negative that I took two weeks annual leave after just nine months. Physically, emotionally and spiritually I was exhausted. After two weeks away, I had prepared a sermon for my first day back. The night before however, I had a panic attack. I could not face going back. I paced around our unit, not able to get my breath and not wanting to wake Dimity. Sleep was out of the question. At one point I remember saying to God: I don't want to go back. I would rather die. Please take me now. I looked out of the third storey window and the thought of jumping even crossed my mind.

The next morning, I somehow managed to get dressed and arrive at church in time. But when it came time for the message, I put my sermon notes aside and I shared with the church exactly what had happened the night before and how I was feeling.

We had a small wooden cross on the platform. I picked it up, as I was sharing about my preference to die. I declared that I had died to self and would take up the cross and follow Jesus regardless of the outcomes, or of the emotions or of the experiences. I invited anyone to come forward who was also willing to die to self. Everyone came forward. We cried together, we prayed together and then we sang together. That was the beginning of the healing, and it was a new start for the church. Some families were not present that day, and interestingly, they left soon after. Sometimes a new environment is needed for healing to take place.

A fresh wind blew through the remaining church family. We no longer looked back. New ministries began. Fiona, a very gifted special education teacher, started a playgroup for local mums. We connected with the local primary school and together with their principal, Shirley, started a Friday afternoon youth group for those in their final year of primary school or their first year of secondary school. We also worked closely with the school to present community Christmas events.

The young adults who had been faithful in their weekly Bible studies now started a Sunday night café church. The whole church embarked on a 'Train to Proclaim' course with evangelist Stuart Millar. Enthusiasm and joy returned. New people started to come, and they were loved, valued and included.

We continued to clean and develop the property. The original church building was rented out to another church. Two rooms were designated for the playgroup and an outdoor playground was erected. The babies' room was beautifully renovated, and the youth had their own designated room. Church was held in a big shed that had never had its ceiling or walls lined. The stage was a temporary platform set on Besser bricks. The carpet was threadbare, and the laminated wooden pews were shedding their laminate. We now had an income from our tenants, so we embarked on a complete renovation.

God was the renovator. Mobile Missions Maintenance had a three-week window in which they could come and provide labour. We demolished the temporary stage, cleared out the old carpet and pews and began from scratch. The high ceiling was completed with colour bond sheeting and an installed projector. The walls were fully lined from floor to ceiling. A new stage was erected, complete with wings and a mezzanine floor. The walls were plastered and painted. New carpet and tiles were laid, and new pews installed. The entrance was also beautifully decorated. From beginning to end it took just three weeks. We all stood back and just marvelled.

Now after four years, the church building not only looked beautiful, the Body of Christ was also healthy and purposeful. Having fought so many battles, I was now ready to enjoy ministry.

God had other ideas.

I don't know if I was born a fighter, but I certainly became a fighter early on in life. It seems usual that our spiritual life develops in parallel with our disposition. Impulse is a natural trait in our lives, but God has so much more for us and our character, personality and temperament. He takes us from our childlike impulses and allows us to develop intuition. This necessitates hardships and challenges. It also necessitates a steadfast knowledge that God is able. He is sufficient. His all-sufficiency is not to give us the kind of life we have always craved. It is much greater and more exhilarating than that. He gives us Himself. He is our shield, our very great reward.

Part Two
The Teaching Spirit

But the Advocate, the Holy Spirit, whom the Father will send in My name will teach you all things and will remind you of everything I have said to you.

John 14:26

11

A Foretaste in Missions

Back in January 2002, I had been asked to go on a trip to Solomon Islands.[7] Someone else had planned to go but because of family circumstances, they needed to withdraw at the last minute. The Solomon Island Wesleyan Women were holding their first-ever convention and I was to be one of the two speakers. It was such a bonus to accompany Gwen Akers on this trip. Gwen, and her husband Ray, had been ministering in Solomon Islands for several years. They had also worked for many years on the mission field in Papua New Guinea. While I knew nothing about Solomon Islands, Gwen was familiar with Melanesian culture and language.

We were met at the little island airport on Nusa Tupe that serviced the islands of the central western province of Solomon Islands. The women presented us with floral leis and cold green coconuts to drink. They then accompanied us in a motorised canoe, over to Gizo. Gizo is the second biggest town in the Solomons and at that time, had twenty-eight shops, some roads and electricity. PT109 was a café and wharf named after John F Kennedy's patrol boat that had been torpedoed nearby in World War II. This famous story tells of the heroism of JFK and of Solomon Islanders who were crucial in the rescue of the crew. The owner of this establishment was a big man in town, Lawrie Wickham. He was a descendant of one of the first Englishmen to come to Solomons as a trader. He had been a national politician and was held in high regard. In fact, he was one of the men who signed the document giving Solomon Islands independence from Great Britain. The way he spoke to Morina led me to think that she must have been his house girl. He certainly presented as the boss. Only later did I realise that Morina was, in fact, the National Director of Wesleyan Women and was one of the main organisers of the entire event.

We stayed with the pastor of the Gizo Church, Hall Malasa, and his beautiful family. News had spread that Gwen and I were in town for the night, so naturally a church service was quickly convened. The next day we met Helena, an elderly woman who lived on the other side of the island and who had walked many kilometres to visit us. She had been unable to make the journey at night. Gwen proceeded to tell her about the message from the church service. Helena stopped her. It seemed like she remembered the whole message better than I did and she wasn't even there. Helena explained that she had met a man on the road that morning who had been to church and who told her all about the service. I was markedly impressed.

We gathered back at the PT109 wharf to get into a motorised canoe for travel to the village of Maravari on the island of Vella la Vella. Women travelled from all directions to attend. Many walked from their villages, some paddled traditional dugout canoes and others came like us, in a motorised canoe. It was such a joy to be amongst these amazing women. Each church had made special dresses for the women to wear, and the convention commenced with the representatives marching around the village in their uniforms.

During the first session the women were given an opportunity to introduce themselves. Each woman gave her name, where she was from, where her husband was from and how many children she had. These each expressed an essential aspect of their identity. They were very surprised when I revealed that I only had one child and, in fact, had never been married.

Every leader had worked very hard to prepare for the convention and their organisation was impeccable. It came as a great shock to me to see that the men simply took over. They ignored the program planned by the women and decided that it was they who needed to chair the meetings. The male District Secretary took minutes, and the male District Superintendent chaired the meetings. Although these decisions had nothing to do with me, I was offended on behalf of the women. My resentment towards the men came from my world perspective and I therefore saw it as interference. So it came as a surprise to me that, the women did not complain but with quiet grace and submission, allowed the men to change all of their plans. So taken back was I that I asked the leaders, Gloria and Morina, how they were coping with the men changing their plans. Gloria responded that they would just accept what the men were doing without complaint. God settled my spirit with a gentle reminder, "You are not here to change culture. You are here to preach the Word." This was such an important lesson for me to learn.

Nothing could dampen the enthusiasm of the women who had travelled far and wide to attend the convention. Everyone was touched in some way by the events of that week. At the conclusion of the convention, the man who had chaired the meetings stood up and said, "We now see that you women can run your own convention and that you will not need us next time." Some men did come to the next Women's convention. However, they came to do the cooking, cleaning and child minding, allowing the women the freedom to enjoy their time together and to manage their own program.

Gwen and I returned to Gizo by motorised canoe and again were warmly welcomed by Hall and Dorah Malasa. We had one day's rest before flying back to Australia. However, word again had spread that there were two *missionaries* in town. People came asking for prayer. I was expecting Gwen to take the lead because of her experience, but so many came that we each took a different room in the house to meet with those desiring prayer.

Listening to the critical needs, I felt completely inadequate. Thankfully, I knew that God was not inadequate and that nothing was impossible with Him. Again surprising to me, and observing prayer requests were often preceded by a time of confession. After reading Scripture, witnessing confession, forgiveness and reconciliation taking place; I often forgot the details of the initial prayer request. This was an especially humbling time and a great reminder of God's love, mercy and power.

Returning home meant that my new ministry was to begin immediately. How quickly the lessons I had learnt were relegated to the back of my mind.

My second trip to the Solomons came in January 2004. Because I had been before, I was asked if I would be willing to lead a team to go over and run a youth convention. This was to be their first national youth convention and having had such an amazing time with the women, I was more than happy to return. I was able to go because it was my holiday time. Our team of seven prepared resources to run a mini-Olympics with the youth. I knew from my experience teaching physical education that these types of activities were always enjoyable and I was sure they would cross cultural boundaries in an Olympic year.

We travelled from Honiara to Gizo by plane and then by motorised canoe to the island of Ranunga. This is a large island close to Vella la Vella but perhaps not as populated. We arrived at the village of Olelavata. This was a small, isolated community on top of a cliff. The youth convention in this location was only possible because of a remarkable young man named Nakalo. Nakalo was in his mid-twenties and the son of the District Superintendent, Richard. Nakalo had spent a year in Olelavata preparing for the convention. He cleared jungle, planted gardens, built a church building and a house for the seven little Australians. When I asked his father Richard, if Nakalo was married. He replied, "No, he is only a boy." To my surprise others also treated him like a boy and the respect that I thought he was due, seemed to be missing.

Canoes came from every direction, and we had over two hundred gather for this great week of fellowship, fun and faith building. I was impressed with a not-so-young youth leader called Bilder who shone at every activity and whose enthusiasm was contagious.

An earnest young man named Ambrose sought me out for advice about his life situation. It was such a surprise to be trusted and to pray with him for God's guidance, strength and wisdom. One night I was woken up to go to a girl who was suffering severe abdominal pain. Her youth group were sleeping under a makeshift tarp erected over branches cut from the jungle. It was pitch black and I couldn't really see anyone, but I knew the space was crowded.

The young girl had a high fever and was in agony with pain in her right side. I suspected it might be appendicitis. We only had a basic first aid kit and there was no way that that we could move her let alone transport her to Gizo hospital by canoe in the dark. It was a desperate situation.

My mind went back to that amazing day of prayer in Gizo two years earlier. All that I could remember of James Chapter 5 I spoke out loud. I confessed that I was not worthy. Spontaneously, many of the young ones present, began confessing and asking God for forgiveness. There were many tears. When a rational moment returned, I was able to anoint the young girl with oil and pray for her healing. Somehow, we all returned to our beds and slept soundly. The next morning, I didn't have to ask how she was. She was up and running around, ready to participate in all of the activities and smiling from ear to ear.

One of the great joys of the youth convention was seeing the interaction between young people who had previously not met each other. The other standout memory for me was the powerful dramas each group presented. Their creativity and talent was truly amazing and it was obvious to me that they had received great leadership. Our team had previously decided to split up at the conclusion of this fabulous week. Being so close to Maravari, I wanted to return and greet those who had previously hosted me so well. Kasia and Nicky came with me. Kasia had been a part of the Woodridge Youth Group and was now a youth leader in her church. It was such a joy to be on this trip together. Nicky was a new Christian, full of enthusiasm, love for God and love for others.

The plan was for the other four to return to Gizo and for us all meet to up in twenty-four hours, ready to return home. There was a report of a cyclone brewing. We set out for Maravari early, hoping to avoid any rough seas. I remember getting into the heavily laden canoe thinking: Wow! They must be very good navigators. This confidence, however, was quickly shattered.

The cloud cover meant we could not see anything in any direction. We had not gone very far when the canoe stopped, and an argument ensued among the men as to which direction they needed to go. A young girl stood up in the front of the canoe and confidently pointed in a direction that she believed we should go. She was promptly ignored. We set off again but found ourselves going right into the teeth of the gale.

The swell was building and now the canoe struggled to get over each swell, only to then be thumped down with a thud in just enough time to face the next wave. The seasoned travellers were throwing up over the side of the canoe, as were Kasia and Nicky. I knew that Kasia could not swim and began to worry for her safety. The canoe changed direction to go with the wind. There was a break in the sky long enough to reveal the outline of an island. With the identification of this island came the realisation that we were way off course. We took shelter on a small, uninhabited island where we spent many hours waiting for an improvement in the weather.

Finally, we were able to set off for Maravari, arriving close to dark. The people had been patiently waiting for our arrival all day and had prepared a marvellous feast. Unfortunately, no one had much of an appetite. Another canoe was expected to travel from Olelavata. When I inquired about this other canoe, I was told that it would not have travelled in such dangerous seas and would return tomorrow. I was further told that people died on that particular route. I believe that they only travelled because we had a schedule, which they felt obliged to keep.

I remember wishing that I knew more and understood more. I also wished that we visitors would not be treated differently to the locals but that we could be one in all circumstances. I felt that we had unknowingly put their lives in danger.

The return to Australia and fulltime ministry was once again all consuming, but I treasured my time in the Solomons and the inspirational people I had met there.

Good Friday 2006 saw me spend a day alone with God. Good Friday is the most special day of the year for me, a time to reflect and ponder God's love. As I sat on a rock overlooking the ocean, I found myself thinking about an email, concerning the Solomons, from Ray and Gwen. They were finishing up their itinerant teaching ministry there and were asking for volunteers to go over and do some teaching. Because I had been so impacted by my two visits and I loved to teach, I thought that maybe I could go over every two years, make it a working holiday, and do some teaching. I then amended my thinking to the possibility of even going annually. As I was having these thoughts, God spoke to me saying, "This is not an added-on extra. This is it."

The renovated and renewed church was now going well and the thought of leaving to take an unknown ministry in the Solomon Islands was not something I was pursuing. After that Easter, I attended a pastor's retreat where the District Superintendent, Lex Akers, preached a challenging message from Jeremiah Chapter 12. He pointed out that there was so much more we could be doing for the Kingdom of God. The verse in which the Lord says, "If you have raced on foot against men and they have worn you out, how will you be able to compete with horses?"[8]

I had battled and persevered to a place where I now could enjoy ministry. However, I knew that I could not stay in a place of safety and security when God had so much more for me to do. It became evident that I needed to follow up and make myself available to go to the Solomons fulltime. I went straight from that session to meet with Ray and Gwen and to share God's call. We embraced, cried and prayed and they supported and encouraged me in every step of my journey.

12

The Background Mission Field Solomon Islands

The small nation of Solomon Islands is best known for being the site of strategic battlefields, on land and sea, during World War II. These include the battles of Guadalcanal: at sea on what is now known as Iron Bottom Sound, and on land at what became known as the Thin Red Line, separating the Japanese from the Allies. The battles that raged throughout the Solomons and the Coral Sea came to be crucial turning points in the Pacific arena. Previous to this, little was known about the tiny nation of Solomon Islands

It is a country made up of over 900 islands with, at most, one third being inhabited. Rich in natural resources on both land and sea, it gained its independence from Great Britain on July 7, 1975. The eight provinces are distinct geographically and each has their own languages. Previous to Christian influence, fierce battles raged between islands. War canoes were constructed for raids. Stories of cannibalism and headhunting are legendary.

Ironically, Christian mission came as a result of the barbaric practice of *blackbirding*. Western traders came in their ships to the Solomons and abducted natives to work in the cane fields of Queensland and Fiji. Methodist missionaries had long been active in Fiji, then in Tonga and then Samoa.

The Solomon Islanders who found themselves taken to work in Fiji, observed that there was one day of the week on which no work was done. People gathered together in churches on this day. The Solomon Islanders were initially attracted to the singing coming from those churches. Over time, many responded to the Gospel. These men and women had lost everything, their freedom, their homes, their families, and their place in tribal communities. While now they had hope for eternity, they still had grave concern for the families they had left behind in their home villages.

From 1875 to 1900, some letters were written to the Australian Mission Society pleading with that organisation to send missionaries to Solomon Islands. Such a venture was considered too dangerous until the General Secretary of the mission, Dr. George Brown, decided he would travel to the Solomons himself. This trip began in 1899. He connected with two English traders in the Roviana Lagoon, Francis Wickham and Norman Wheatley. These men had built a relationship with the chiefs of the Roviana Lagoon in order to carry out their trading, and there seemed a possibility that missionaries may be able to settle in the area.

Dr. Brown travelled to the now established Methodist Bible College in Fiji, to recruit candidates for the mission field. He spoke to the students about Solomon Islands, warning them clearly of the dangers they would face there. He asked the students to go home and pray about the possibility of their going. All returned the next day and when Dr. Brown asked if any felt that God was calling them to go to Solomon Islands, every one of the eighteen students stood up prepared to go. Six Fijian and three

Tongan students were selected. The participants were given every opportunity to change their minds and not be a part of this new venture. This is how they responded.

We wish to inform your Honour that this is no new thing to us. We were fully and carefully informed of the dangers which may be incurred from the cannibal propensities of the natives of those islands and the insalubrious nature of the climate which produces fever and ague, and diseases of that character, as well as discomforts we may undergo from want of the food to which we are accustomed, and from not being able to speak the language of the people, among whom we should be left without protection or support for many months. No one appointed us to go. After consultation we decided to volunteer, and we are thankful to God that we have been selected for this great work. No one has pressed us in any way; we have given ourselves up to do God's work, and our mind today, sir, is to go with Mr. Brown. If we die, we die; if we live, we live.[9]

The team arrived in May 1902. The Rev. John Francis Goldie, a Wesleyan Methodist minister from Tasmania was nominated to be the leader of the team. Universally remembered as Goldie, he was thirty-one years of age. His young wife Helena was not permitted to join the initial team. However, she joined her husband one year later and stayed for twenty years. Goldie stayed for fifty years.

Helena was a nurse and Goldie had a teaching background. Education and health became the foundations of their ministry. John started to teach young boys to read and write, while Helena was of great assistance to the women, especially during and after the birth of babies. Mr Wheatley and Mr Wickham paved the way for the missionaries by establishing relationships of tolerance with the chiefs of Roviana.

Soon after settling at Kokenglo, John Goldie asked one of these chiefs, "Why do you go and raid Choiseul so much?" The chief replied with a question. "If we don't kill them who will?"[10]

After five years, Goldie reported that there were 500 attending services in Roviana and 5000 throughout the Western Province but none of these professed to be a Christian.[11]

Outwardly, attendance records could give the impression that the mission was very successful, however, it was only when conversions were powerfully experienced that real transformation of the human experience took place. This was particularly true in regard to victory over fear-based practices. It is also of interest that the missionaries did not rush the sacrament of baptism following conversion, but, rather, had the new Christians undergo twelve months of discipleship before being baptised.

The Gospel brought light to this nation, causing a turning away from headhunting and cannibalism. Villages moved closer to the sea, now that there was no danger from raiding parties. Churches were established in every village. A handful of missionaries could not have physically accomplished this amazing transformation alone. The oral traditions allowed the people themselves to tell the stories wherever they went. I witnessed that first-hand when I first met Helen in Gizo back in 2002.

The great chief of the Western Solomons, Ingava, strongly opposed the mission at its commencement but ended up becoming their sincere friend. He had been ill for some time and the missionaries, primarily Helena Goldie, nursed him with tenderness and care. Not long before he died in 1906, he tried to express his thanks for all they had done for him. However, when it was known that Ingava was dead, there was an outbreak of old customs. The leading woman of Vella la Vella was sacrificed so that Ingava might not go alone on his long journey into the unknown. Two girls from a distant village, who had declared their intention of going to the mission station for training, were killed and eaten by their own tribe.[12]

Against this background the spirit of the Lotu (gospel) was like a fire that nothing could quench, and the greater the persecution the greater it grew. It seemed possible that new believers could lay down fear-based customs and superstitions and sincerely worship the true God. The Goldies observed changed lives and a totally new way of living emerging.

> At one such meeting an old man who had been baptised the previous month rose to his feet and briefly told his story. Many years ago the Roviana warriors attacked the hill village where he lived and in the slaughter that followed all of the one hundred and fifty inhabitants were killed except for himself and three others. Some of those invaders were present in the class meeting that day. The young teacher who had led him to Christ was the son of one of those savages [sic] who had wiped out his village. Only in Christ can there be complete reconciliation.[13]

As the missionaries were more and more tolerated, they set out to other islands spreading the Gospel to new communities. Churches were established on Simbo, Vella la Vella, Ranunga, Choiseul and Bougainville. Helena had such an impact upon the people that the two largest hospitals in Solomon Islands are named after her. John Goldie's commitment of fifty years, his diligence in learning the Roviana language, translating the Scriptures and training indigenous pastors, saw him universally held in high regard.

Going to Solomon Islands fifty years after John Goldie left, I made an observation that in some places, the knowledge, understanding and power of the gospel had been, to a large extent, replaced with a culture of *doing church*. Such appearance of Christianity, without the ongoing power and presence of the Holy Spirit is not uncommon throughout the evangelised world.

In the midst of this perceived environment, however, there was genuine faith in God. Ray and Gwen's ministry had heightened a desire for knowledge and understanding. Hall Malasa volunteered to be the boat driver as they travelled around different islands. One of the many reasons I respect Hall is because he shared with me that he had not always been the best man he could be, but there was something in his life that drew him to want to learn of God. Many people do not have this level of humility. As Hall had the opportunity to sit in on many classes, his life began to change. He was soon enthusiastically attending every class and every church service. Before long he was appointed as pastor of the Gizo Church and he thrived in ministry. He visited the hospital and the prison, as well as the homes of the churchgoers. He became an accomplished preacher, counsellor and guide. Supported and encouraged by his wife Dorah, he attended the Bougainville Bible College and eventually became National Superintendent and the second person ordained in the Wesleyan Methodist Church of Solomon Islands.

13
White is Only Skin Deep

On my previous visits to Solomon Islands, I had learnt that westerners were referred to as *white men*. It did not matter if you were male or female, so I was referred to as a *white man*. Those from a Polynesian background, whose skin was not as black as the Melanesians, were referred to as "Palangi". Even within the different tribes and different islands there was variation in skin colour. I still found it surprising to sometimes hear one person describing another as "the one with black skin."

Before commencing in January 2007, in September 2006, I travelled there for a planning trip. I met with the national leaders, again at the village of Maravari. Fiona, one of the leaders from my church travelled with me. We found it awkward at mealtimes to have our food set up in a room by ourselves with a table and two chairs. Everyone else sat on the grass outside and fellowshipped together over their meal. Gloria, who I first met in 2002, brought us our food. Maravari was her home village. Although she had married and moved away, her parents and many family members still lived in Maravari. I asked Gloria if we, too, could go outside and sit on the grass for our meals. She seemed embarrassed at the prospect, on behalf of the people. We then asked if she would be willing to join us and that again seemed like an unrealistic request. Although we both felt awkward sitting up there on our own, we also understood that the hosting of *white men* was a new and somewhat uncomfortable experience for them.

This became all the more obvious when I travelled alone to some of the more isolated villages. Several of the villages had never had a white person come to stay before. Babies cried and some children hid. Other children boldly came and lifted up my clothes to see if I was white all over.

Gizo became my home base, and I was blessed to be able to stay in town with Hall and Dorah and their family. From their grandchildren I learned Pijin, which is a specific dialect of Solomon Islands, and not to be confused with Pidgin English. It was wonderful to be treated as one of the family and trusted enough to mind their granddaughter, small Dorah, for a month when they travelled away for Hall's ministry.

By the time Dorah and I travelled to Supezei ready to embark on a mission tour to North Choiseul, we were close friends. The Choiseul District Superintendent, Jefferson, his wife Doris, and elder Jack Provan completed the team. I had never met Doris before and although she had a need for prayer before the trip began, she would not come and talk to me about it or even look at me. Dorah acted as intermediary. At each village, women and men were accommodated separately. Doris took Dorah aside after the first night and asked how it was that she was laughing and being friends with a white man. Dorah explained that I was like a sister to her. To my great joy, by the end of our event-filled tour, Doris and I had become firm friends.

Eating separately soon became a distant memory. In every village I had the joy of eating with all of the locals and course participants, while we were sitting on the grass together. Travelling across the ocean in canoes, cargo ships or chartered vessels, in all kinds of weather, soon meant that wherever I went I was welcomed the same as my Melanesian brothers and sisters.

I didn't realise that I had forgotten about my skin colour until an incident at Supezei. I had spent a month, teaching various courses in this beautiful small village. There was much excitement in the village one day, and everyone ran to the seaside. Some of the students and I wondered what the fuss was about. "White man!" was the cry. A white man in a canoe was paddling into the village. I got up and ran with the others who were excitedly calling, "White man!" It was only when I was halfway there that I was hit with the realisation: Hang on a minute. I am a white man.

Some years after my retirement, I went back to the Solomons for the Ordination of Gloria Philip and Richard Solomon Soto. I had known these two godly people for a long time and always said that I would go back for their ordination. The afternoon before the ordination service, George Velopide, the National Superintendent came to me and asked if I would preach at the service in the morning.

According to the program, it was George who was to preach. I said that I would not do that. He was the National Superintendent and the people needed to see their leader preaching at this significant service. He was insistent, so I asked if we could meet with the national board after the evening service so that I could speak to them. I did not want to dishonour George by declining his invitation and I wanted to explain to the board why I was declining. It was after ten-thirty that night before we were able to meet together. I explained that having a white man come and preach at such an important service was against my whole philosophy of mission.

My rationale for not accepting the invitation to preach was driven by my belief that having a *white man* preach at such an important occasion was counter productive to the goal of endorsement. From the beginning, my intention was to provide education, enable nationals to be empowered and, more importantly, to endorse their leadership. I concluded my ministry primarily because I believed in their ability, giftedness and calling. It would be counterproductive for me to come back and preach. I expected the board and George to accept my argument and that there would be agreement and understanding with no hard feelings. George asked that we go around the circle, and everyone express his or her opinion. This is the usual practice for Melanesian decision making. Every member of the Board expressed their desire for me to take the message. It was their reasoning that shook my world.

"Zai Kay, you are not a "*white man*". You lived with us. You've shared our life. You are one of us and we want you to preach."

There were many tears as we hugged, prayed and sang together. I didn't get back to my accommodation until close to midnight, when I suddenly realised that I had to come up with a message in ten hours' time. God undertook. Julie, Rose and Cindy had travelled to the conference from Wangaratta, a city in the northeast of Victoria. They were working with the women while I spent my time with the youth. As I got back to the house where we were all staying, I noticed that their light was still on and they were awake. I went in and shared with them what had happened. They prayed with me and as we talked and prayed, it seemed that God gave me the message that He wanted me to preach. The next day, I delivered, in Pijin, the message I had prepared in English. For a short moment in time I felt a transcendence of culture.

14
Goals, Tasks and Outcomes

It was twelve years earlier that I had begun my formal ministry in Solomon Islands. I was a novice in cross-cultural ministry and not even aware of my shortcomings. Facing the challenges of life and ministry, together with studies at the Summer Institute of Linguistics in Melbourne, was solid preparation. However, even though I went as a teacher, I immediately realised how much I had to learn. My teachers came in the form of men, women and children of all ages in many different villages.

When God called me to go to Woodridge, it was indeed the last place on earth that I wanted to go. However, in reality, I belonged there. I had lived there from two years of age until I turned twenty-one. I knew the history. I knew many people and if they did not know me, they knew my mother or my father or one of my brothers. I attended the primary school. I taught at the primary school. When I went back to pioneer a church, I went back as a single mother. I fitted in and I was accepted as an equal who knew what it was like to have to deal with Centrelink[14] and its accompanying prejudices.

When God called me to go to Solomon Islands, I was delighted. It was the fulfilment of a twenty-year dream to be a missionary. However, in reality, I did not belong there. For a start, I had white skin. I only spoke English and I knew nothing of the Melanesian culture and worldview.

The planning week of September 2006 was crucial to the direction of my ministry. I entered into a culture that was not time or task oriented, but rather, focused on the present. It took me longer to understand the consequences of the indirect nature of the Melanesian culture that were in contrast to the directness of the West. My ignorance of both of these facts was astounding. I came from a culture that was focused on the future with an underlying mindset of continuous growth and improvement.

All of my education had incorporated goals, strategies, rationales, outcomes, and key performance indicators. When I asked the leaders what their immediate and future goals were, I was thinking like a Westerner and showing my ignorance of Melanesian culture. Thankfully they were gracious to me. It took that week of sitting on the grass and listening to the leaders speak about their concerns for their church, for me to understand that they wanted all their pastors to be qualified. While people had benefited from Ray and Gwen's teaching, there were many pastors who had no formal training. There was a great desire for more teaching. Many of the pastors who had been chosen by the leadership of their tribe had no formal training at all.

I was given the task of formulating a curriculum that pastors could work through, in order to become licenced ministers. To be a licenced minister in the Wesleyan Methodist Church, a candidate needs to have completed a curriculum of nine theological subjects. They also need to be under the guidance of the Board of Ministerial Development that will interview them and monitor their progress. They can then be appointed as a pastor to a local church. The licensing is only valid for the duration of their appointment, but it allows them to preach, chair local church meetings, carry out baptisms, weddings, funerals and other pastoral ministries.

To become an ordained minister, the process is more rigorous and includes the completion of twenty-four subjects, proven practical experience and evaluation of gifts and graces. The immediate goal set by the national leaders was to have all of their pastors qualify to be licenced ministers.

Before finishing up their ministry, Ray and Gwen Akers had scheduled a visit, in January 2007, to Supezei, a small village on the northern tip of the large island of Choiseul. During the planning week in Maravari, we decided together that this schedule would be kept, but rather than being just for Choiseul participants, pastors from Vella and Central West districts would be encouraged to travel and join in this training. The January dates and location for our first formal period of training were now confirmed.

I returned to Australia to make preparations for these courses and future training.

I presumed that arrangements had been agreed to for the hosting of this course. Unfortunately, there were no representatives from Choiseul present at these planning meetings. Two things I had no understanding of were, the difficulty with communication between islands and the challenges of travelling from one district to another over the seas.

I had the advantage of arriving at Supezei by plane and canoe, rather than an exhaustive ship journey, on the last day of 2006. Eighteen students had travelled by ship from the west of Solomon Islands to Supezei. As it happened, there was a passenger ship travelling the route from Gizo to Supezei at just the required time. There was much excitement at being together and being hosted by the small church at Supezei. The visitors from Vella and the Central West, together with the Choiseul group meant that we had thirty-five keen participants.

After celebrating the start of the New Year, we met for the commencement of formal classes on January 1, 2007. I was very excited and there was an air of anticipation amongst the students. Jason Doromolovo was the District Superintendent of Choiseul and also the chief of Supezei. As I sat in the front seat of the church building, his opening words of greeting took me by surprise.

Jason said, "When I was asked if I would host the course here my first response was, No." Jason was a man held in very high regard. He was well educated, wise and accomplished. He had been a member of parliament and one of the elite Solomon Islanders who had signed the documents for the country to gain its independence from Great Britain. Jason went on to state that he did not want any more "whitemen" coming to Solomon Islands.

"We have had whitemen coming for ten years and we do not even have any members. What is the point?" he questioned.

Then I was introduced to begin the class.

That was not the most affirming introduction I had ever received. Nonetheless, there was a sense of excitement about the proposed course of study. Apart from the classes, the degree of fellowship we experienced was extraordinary. Previously, no one could name all the churches, let alone the pastors of those churches. We got into the habit of praying for all of the churches and during the two weeks together we shared stories and built strong bonds of friendship. One of the delights of this first combined course was presenting an opportunity to get to know each other and to have prayer partnerships form.

The basic Theology course included a formal membership component, which was just as well, considering Jason's comments.

It was delightful that Jason would question me often during the course. His well-reasoned arguments were a catalyst for enthusiastic class discussions. These interactions caused us all to think deeply and to search the Scriptures more thoroughly. The second week focused on 'The Spiritual Battle'. I did not know at the time how significant this course would turn out to be and am thankful for Denis Hartin's willingness to formulate the course and take many trips to the Solomons to teach this and other subjects. Denis was a pastor on the Sunshine Coast of Queensland and had a Solomon Islander in his congregation. As this woman, Hine, sat under Denis's teaching, she knew that his insights would be highly valued in her homeland.

The five districts in the Solomon Islands Wesleyan Methodist Church are Honiara, New Georgia, Vella, Choiseul, and Central West. If you look at a map you will see that the Central West District includes Gizo, Simbo, Ranunga, Kolambangara and Mono.

At this first joint course we had students from Choiseul, Central West and Vella. The next combined course was held at Maravari in Vella and delegates from New Georgia were able to travel by canoe to join. Unfortunately, those who lived in Honiara were unable to join in the courses held in the west because of the huge distances involved and the expense of travel. Eventually all courses could also be taught in Honiara.

Over the next three years we were able to deliver the nine subjects required for licencing to all five districts. Because of the difficulties with travel, there was only one combined course a year. I would travel to each district to deliver the other courses. For the combined courses, there would often be a team come from Australia to assist with tutoring. Guest lecturers were also included in the program. Joan Guscott came to teach Counselling. Joan and her husband John had for many years been missionaries in Bougainville.

Joan had also visited Solomons on many occasions as her daughter and son in law were involved in Bible translation into the Gela language of the Nggela (Florida) Islands in Central Province. It was great to have someone so familiar with Melanesian culture come to teach.

After three years there were twelve students who became Licenced Ministers. It was then possible to introduce the subjects needed for ordination. Four more years of the mobile Bible College saw the first group of students presented for ordination.

15
Trials of Travels

One of the great thrills of teaching in many different locations was that not only pastors attended courses, but also anyone who was able to would make the effort to attend. For some, they may only be able to complete one course. Others started to travel to attend as many courses as they could. The courses were always open to anyone from any denomination.

Travelling to courses brought many challenges for all of us. After some testing and trying trips, I started to rate the sea voyages out of ten, depending on the weather, ocean swells, currents, size of engine, mechanical difficulties and length of travel. A rating of one meant a perfect trip on glassy seas, sometimes accompanied by dolphins. I enjoyed a bit of a swell so a rating of three or four meant they were good trips.

The only trip I rated ten out of ten was life threatening and coincided with a visit from Dimity who was then preparing for her wedding. We were travelling around Vella, staying one night in each village. We were on the western side of the island at Supato and scheduled to travel back around the island to Kenepide for the opening of their new church building.

Thankfully we had Watson Otota as our boat driver, and he had a seventy-five-horsepower engine. It was another occasion when travel would not have been undertaken without the presence of *white men* and their schedules. The swells were so severe that we should not have been on the sea. The open canoe with five aboard could not climb the ten-metre swells. Timing was everything. After the canoe crested the swell, we then had to ride across the top of it and then time accurately the descent back down to sea level. Thankfully Watson decided to pull into a nearby village and take shelter.

I remember thinking that I didn't mind dying but I did not want to witness my daughter drown. I looked down at Dimity on the floor of the canoe as we descended with a huge thump from one of our failed attempts to conquer the swells. As I feared for her safety and her wellbeing, there she was smiling at what she thought was a great adventure. I asked her later, "Weren't you afraid?" "No." she said. "I knew I could swim to shore if we were thrown out." In those seas it would have been a huge struggle just to stay afloat and breathe, let alone swim anywhere. I was pleased for her naïve confidence and lack of worry.

It was not only rough seas that made travel from island to island challenging. Engine failure, lack of paddles, water in the petrol, and lengths of time out in the hot sun all brought their challenges. But there were also great blessings. When a flight scheduled between Gizo and Choiseul was cancelled due to lack of petrol, we were faced with a nine-hour canoe voyage. People have died on this voyage, which can be very dangerous. However, the sea was fine, and we almost ran into a sleeping dolphin at daybreak.

The most spectacular journey came on an early morning trip from Gizo to Soneke in South Choiseul. We left Gizo in the dark and were delighted by the most amazing sunrise in the middle of the ocean. I had lost any sense of direction but understood that we had to be travelling north; I had a sense that the beautiful colours were not in the east. As I turned my head and looked around the ocean, I discovered a complete 360-degree sunrise of spectacular colours. It was an awe-inspiring moment in time during which I felt close to God and His amazing creation.

Travelling by canoe from Gizo to Munda, on the island of New Georgia, was a truly beautiful experience. With such skill, boat drivers navigate the reefs giving time to sit back and enjoy the ride. In the District of New Georgia is the Morovo Lagoon. It is the largest saltwater lagoon in the world. Divers come from all over the world to enjoy these magnificent waters. There were many visits to the churches at Kolotepe, Vogi and Rarumana where each church building had spectacular elements either because of its proximity to the beach, or because of the magnificent views from its hilltop position.

I have been privileged to climb a live volcano called Ove on the island of Simbo, and also to traverse the island of Kolombangara witnessing the remnants of giant clams big enough for me to sit in. There was a day spent in pouring rain near the wharf at Ringi, waiting for a truck to take us across the island. The rain eventually stopped and we piled into the back of a truck packed with workers returning home. As we drove through pristine jungles ascending the impressive Mount Veve, I remember sitting in the back of a flatbed truck reflecting on my recent travels and thinking: You would pay big money to be having these travel experiences with someone you love. Then I realised that was exactly what I *was* doing.

Students went to great lengths to be able to attend courses. One annual combined course was scheduled for Dunde on the island of New Georgia. This was a particularly long journey for the Choiseul students. So determined were they to attend, that they loaded their canoe even though the only engine they could acquire was a mere six horsepower. I was used to travelling with at least a forty horsepower engine, in which case this trip would have taken six hours. They crossed the ocean and followed the shoreline of Vella la Vella and then down to Gizo before they could enter the more sheltered waters into the Roviana Lagoon. It was on the return journey that the ocean turned against them, and they lost their luggage when everyone was thrown out of the canoe. Thankfully no lives were lost.

Stephen lived on Vella la Vella and needed to complete a subject that was being taught at Dunde to become a Licenced Minister. He had no money for a boat fare even to Gizo. So, he decided to paddle. He paddled first to Gizo for a short stopover and then paddled all the way to Munda through the Roviana Lagoon, a distance of over fifty kilometres. By the time he arrived, his hands were in a very bad way, but he was determined that nothing would prevent him from completing his studies.

At another course held in Dunde, Lovelyn Joy Murray was also determined to attend. Joy lived in the village of Vogi, at the other end of the large lagoon. There was no transport to Munda and so she also decided to paddle. Joy paddled all through the night to reach Munda and walked into the first session of the course. She was so exhausted that I arranged for her to go and rest and refresh and come back in the afternoon. Joy was an excellent student and such a faithful worker for God. She became a children's ministry trainer and continues to be an inspiration.

I also experienced a very slow journey in a big canoe with a small engine. Together with Jefferson, who was by then the District Superintendent of Choiseul, we planned a mission trip to the north of Choiseul. There were churches there so isolated that no one had visited for some years.

This trip brought many challenges and again taught me many lessons. There were five of us. Superintendent and now Licenced Minister, Jefferson Qae, his wife Doris, another Choiseul pastor, Jack Provan, and the wife of the National Superintendent and my good friend, Dorah Malasa. Dorah and Doris were both from North Choiseul where the language was slightly different from the language of South Choiseul. I knew that it would be a long journey and suggested that we depart from Supezei early in the morning to avoid the hottest part of the day. We obviously had different interpretations of very early and finally set off just before 10am.

We were travelling so slowly through the smooth passage that took us out to the ocean, that I thought the engine must have another gear. No! That was top speed for the fifteen-horsepower engine. After several hours I began to be affected by the heat. Our engine broke down and it was a kind of relief because it did mean that the women got out of the canoe, swam to shore and walked along the beach as the men paddled. Just before nightfall we came to a tiny village. Although they did not know us, we were welcomed with open arms. The hospitality was amazing as they fed us and gave us a place to sleep after we had all enjoyed a wonderful evening of worship and prayer.

Now fully advised as to where we could get assistance to repair the engine, we set out next morning. It was with great joy that we finally arrived at Sagatumi. I did not know at the time, but I was the first *white man* who had been there. I do know that children would come up to me and lift up my blouse to see if I was white all over. It was such an honour to be amongst the people and to live with them, even for such a short time. The local clinic was without water and only had one mosquito net that was reserved for newborn babies and their mothers. It broke my heart to see the state of the operating theatre and the utter lack of medical supplies and equipment.

From Sagatumi we travelled southeast towards the village of Gagara. This was another very long day with more engine trouble and resultant stopovers for repairs. I met a young girl who was a primary school teacher in her village. She told me how she had failed high school but was accepted as a teacher in her home village because they had no one else available. She had no training at all but was doing the very best she could. Every delay in the journey brought us to a new village and new opportunities to meet local people. By the time we were getting close to Gagarra, it was already dark. Thankfully, Doris and Dorah knew where to go. Again, the hospitality was amazing. We arrived exhausted, wet and hungry and no effort was spared to make us feel welcome and comfortable. Dorah had relatives here, which made the connections even more special. Neither the day of the week nor the hour of the day mattered. Wherever we stopped, we always were blessed to share in worship services and opportunities for prayer.

We were able to visit Sagatumi again on our return journey. The women always slept together on mats on the floor. Early on, Doris took Dorah aside and asked her how she could laugh and have fun with a *"white man"*. Dorah explained that we were friends, like sisters, and that I was the same as them. By the end of the trip Doris and I were also good friends. We certainly did have a lot to laugh about on that memorable journey. I remember seeing the ladies with betel nut shells.[15] I was so shocked because I had never seen Dorah chew betel nut and didn't know why this was happening. When the ladies weren't looking, I threw out the shells, only to find out later that they were using the husks to clean their teeth and not chewing the nuts at all.

After leaving Sagatumi, Jefferson decided to navigate outside of the reef to travel back to Supezei. This meant that we could keep a consistent speed and not worry about the tides and the shallow water over the reef. We were travelling along nicely when I heard a distinct change in the engine. I remember thinking that if it was a car; I would assume we had blown a gasket.

I don't know what happened except, that the engine stopped working completely and we were stuck in the ocean, outside the reef and with no power. I was so impressed with Jefferson's ability to navigate the reef and the waves and get us to shore without capsizing. However, we were now on an isolated island. There were no villages and no one to help. The engine was unrepairable. This was the time for the satellite phone. We were able to contact Billy, the owner of the engine, who lived at Taro. Because of Jack and Jefferson's description, he knew exactly where we were. It took several hours for our rescue, and I was able to use some of the time to swim and collect shells. It was an unexpected and delightful opportunity to sit and story with Dorah and Doris.

I had much to learn about the seasons and the sea so I could start to understand the sensible times to travel and the times to avoid travel. This was essential knowledge in planning any program. I also needed to know the price of petrol and the potential cost of a voyage, dependant for many years on the size of the engine and the number of people in the canoe. It was not easy for me to learn to be a bit more assertive before embarking on a voyage across the ocean. This might have involved checking if the boat driver had paddles, asking for a bigger engine or asking for the trip to be delayed until the conditions improved.

Sometimes it took years of planning to be able to visit the most isolated villages.

16

Mono - Keep the Fire Burning

During 2008, Hall Malasa, now newly ordained as the Wesleyan Church's National Superintendent, received a request from a group on the island of Mono, requesting that the Wesleyan Methodists come to their village. It took two years of communication and planning before this call could be answered. There was much excitement and anticipation when a team was finally able to make the journey.

Mono is a tiny island situated at the north-western extremity of the Solomons. There was one large village of approximately a thousand people. During WWII, the Japanese occupied Mono. They built an airstrip on nearby Stirling Island and began moving their troops south towards Guadalcanal. In late 1943, the Allies, primarily New Zealand troops supported by the United States, landed on Mono, taking the Japanese by surprise. Having secured victory, the Allies were then able to use Mono Island and Stirling Island as launching pads for their advance towards Rabaul. Throughout the village there was still evidence of wartime encounters, including numerous shiny silver fuel tanks from aeroplanes that were now being used as water tanks.

It was difficult and dangerous to travel to Mono by canoe. Solomon Airlines still occasionally used the airstrip on Stirling Island and told us that if we had ten fare-paying passengers, they would fly us there. We were able to raise funds for just five fares, but the airline agreed to the flight. I joined Hall and his wife Dorah, with Ruriko Otota and Kerri Burton completing our team. Kerri had been part of an Australian team that came to Maravari in 2007 and had made several return trips to support the ministry. The chief of Mono, John Goldie, issued an open invitation for us to come to his village. As his name suggests, he had family ties right back to the first Wesleyan Methodists of the early 1900s.

Hall and Dorah were particularly excited about the trip and talked of the great food we would all enjoy. Mono is famous for its coconut crabs, lobsters and fish.

Mono is a very isolated community. Like most of the country's western and northern provinces, it had suffered greatly in the tsunami that followed an undersea earthquake off Gizo in 2007. The people had come together to rebuild damaged and destroyed housing and replace the outrigger canoes that were crucial to their survival. Even though funding was supposed to be available to assist with the rebuilding, the locals knew that being so far from Honiara, and with the money having to travel through so many hands, it was unlikely they would see any of it. Rather than wait for assistance, they worked together to rebuild and replace what had been lost.

Upon our arrival, we went to see Chief Goldie, who welcomed us and encouraged us to hold meetings and classes while we were there. The elders of the village's United Church, who wanted to meet with us, then summoned us. They told us in no uncertain terms that we were not welcome and should not conduct any meetings or classes. We were all in a state of shock. As were the people who had invited us to come.

We were shown to a house where we could stay, and then left alone. We had no food or water and wondered what we were going to do for the week before the plane returned to pick us up. Thankfully, Dorah and Ruriko were very resourceful women and had brought knives with them. They went out scouting to see what they could find for us to eat. Dorah was able to get fire in a coconut shell and bring it to our yard, where she taught me how to keep a fire going with the least amount of wood possible.

That night we organised our own evening devotions in the house we were given. Some of the people who had invited us came, under the cover of darkness, and brought us food. The next day they were bolder and came in daylight. They implored us to take more notice of the chief than of the church elders and to please hold classes and services.

The space beneath one of the houses was made available for us, so we decided to run a Kids' EE (Evangelism Explosion) program. Ruriko and Dorah had been training as Kids' EE teachers, and Kerri had completed the same training in Australia. Many children came during the day, and at night we held services. Towards the end of the week, we received a message via two-way radio that Solomon Airlines would not be coming back to pick us up. Our pleading persuaded them to come the following week and not abandon us since we had already paid return fares.

Here we were with an extra week and were by now feeling more accepted, if not entirely welcome. We decided to run the membership course during the week's delay so people could learn the history, theology and structures of the Wesleyan Methodist Church. The evening services gave opportunities for testimonies that were always preceded by singing. One of the true delights of worshipping in the Solomon Islands was the beautiful singing. Without hymnbooks, the congregation knew every song by heart and choirs would quickly be organised to present items that always enhanced the experience. After one of these night services, when we were back in our house and ready for bed, we heard a knock on the door. Two men were standing outside holding a piece of paper. They told Hall that they wanted to start a Wesleyan Methodist Church in Mono. They had already had a meeting and on the paper, they had written the names of the people who had been chosen to fill the roles of pastor, treasurer, secretary, Sunday school leader and worship leader. They were determined to move ahead despite any opposition they may face.

We all felt that the extra week in Mono had been meant to be, and we were determined to return with others to support the work. Twelve months later we did go back, and this time twenty indigenous students accompanied me. People came both to participate in two courses and to attend the dedication of the church building that the Mono congregation had built.

This time there was no possibility of a flight to Mono. There was, however, a cargo ship, the Biquo 2, travelling from Gizo to Rabaul and stopping at Mono. I was told the journey would be about four hours; in reality, it was nine hours on deck in cyclonic seas. So many people were crammed into the tiny covered section of the deck that we only had one square metre of space each. Thankfully we travelled through the night so we could not actually see the swells, but we certainly felt the effects. Sleeping was difficult. Most of the travellers suffered greatly from seasickness, and some took several days to recover at journey's end.

It was very special to be in Mono for the dedication of the Mono Wesleyan Methodist Church and the installation of their pastor. The courses were well attended and even some people from the other churches participated. We were treated to original drama presentations as students performed their final assessments. This time we were able to explore more of the village. Some of us even enjoyed jumping off the jetty into the crystal-clear water and exploring the caves where coconut crabs could be found. At the conclusion of the courses, I was presented with six freshly caught lobsters, which made our farewell feast very special.

To return to Gizo we had to charter a boat owned by the Gizo Catholic Church. We were again in cramped spaces, but the cyclone had well and truly passed so the seas were calmer. With a much smaller engine though, the trip was long, and we all arrived back exhausted. But we were greatly encouraged by our time spent with our Mono family.

17
Challenging Pests

After returning from Mono, I travelled straight to Dunde for the next round of teaching the New Georgia students. At nights I had an incredibly itchy head that drove me crazy and prevented me from sleeping. Thinking I might have picked up head lice, I managed to find a fine-tooth comb in my luggage. To my horror I discovered that I did not have head lice but there was a colony of fleas living in my hair. There they were, nesting and breeding and having a great time. I experienced a newfound sympathy for any dog that scratches incessantly. After undertaking treatments of insecticide, constant combing, washing and using a coconut oil mixture, I finally got rid of all the invaders. But it took many awful days and nights of discomfort to overcome the infestation.

Solomon Islands has many other remote villages that are difficult to access. It was an enormous adventure and a joy to travel to such locations. None of the difficulties encountered, or opposition faced, ever dampened the enthusiasm of our local leaders to travel and make meaningful connections. When I wasn't teaching, I took every opportunity to visit villages, even if it meant staying just one night there and then moving on. This improved my understanding of daily Solomon life.

On one such visit in my early days, I slept on the floor of a leaf house and was very thankful that I had my mosquito net. The house was not very clean, which was most unusual for Solomon Islands. I concluded that the house was probably not used regularly. They had not received prior warning of my visit, so I was pleased to sleep wherever they could house me. As soon as it was light, I crawled out of my mosquito net and opened the bottom section of my backpack to get out my toiletries. The sight of a rat emerging from it was a complete shock to me. This was my first encounter with a rat, and I did not enjoy it, but there would be many more. It is just a part of life. It was though, a glorious walk, through virgin rainforest beside the ocean, to the next village that ministered to my soul.

That first interaction with the world of rats was just the beginning. Wherever I went, it seemed that rats kept getting too close for comfort. I had always detested rats, a reaction due, at least in part, to hearing stories in school about them carrying the fleas that spread the Great Plague. The idea that rats were the enemy was reinforced by further tales, of convicts being transported to Australia and rats attacking their ears and faces on board the ships. So, to encounter rats firsthand really took me out of my comfort zone. They seemed to be able to get under my mosquito net and crawl up my back during the night. In one conversation by satellite phone with my mission's director in Australia, he asked if I had any specific prayer points, and I answered, "Please pray for a rat-free zone around me." He may have laughed, but I was deadly serious.

Following that request the rat attacks seemed to intensify. I spent a month back at Supezei in Choiseul, sharing my accommodation with a particularly territorial rat. One day I came home from the morning teaching session looking forward to my lunch, only to find the rodent had upended my two bowls and was sitting in my food.

That was the last straw for me. I had been plotting how to get rid of rats and had not been kind in my thinking. Now I went outside the house and spoke to God: What are you trying to teach me God? I know that rats are your creation. I've hated them and I'm sorry for that. Are you saying you want me to love *all* your creation, *including* rats?

I went back inside the house and spoke to the rat. "Rat, I am willing to share this house with you. I just ask one thing, when I am home, please stay away from me. When I am out, you are free to go anywhere you please. Do that and we will get on just fine." I never saw or heard any evidence of the rat again.

When I returned to Gizo and told Dorah my story, she told me that was exactly what they did in her Choiseul culture. Her teaching stayed with me. "The more you try to kill the rat, the more it will annoy you. You need to treat the rat like a queen. Make the rat feel welcome. Then it will leave you alone."

This lesson can surely be applied to more than rats.

18

Food Glorious Food

Villages that hosted courses committed to a huge endeavour in feeding and housing all participants. Once I understood the challenges involved in such an undertaking, I was able to ask the Wesleyan women from my home district in Australia to assist. For many years, they faithfully contributed to the feeding of participants. This meant we could take supplies such as rice, flour, biscuits and tinned goods to every course in supplement of the local gardens.

During a one-week break between courses in the village of Malasova, on the east side of Vella, I was asked to teach some English to the students. We worked in groups of three, sharing in English, the answers to some basic life questions. One of the questions concerned our most favourite and least favourite foods. The universal response was, "There is no food that is not fit for me." While I was longing for chocolate and Coke, cheesecake and banana splits and vegemite, here everyone was grateful for any food. There were never any leftovers. If there was food to eat today, you ate it today. Refrigeration was nonexistent. Sometimes they may need to go without food for a period of time, so you ate whatever was available whenever it was available. The idea of a Melanesian child being a fussy eater was unthinkable. In my years in the Solomons, and despite the lack of Coke and sugar, I never felt hungry.

Eating meals together was always a special time for fellowship. Traditionally, speeches were made during the mealtimes. These were opportunities for expressions of appreciation and reflected the natural free flowing oratory culture. Everyone loved to tell stories, and giving speeches of thanksgiving often took longer than the meal itself.

It took me a while to appreciate the amount of time and effort needed to produce the meals. Firewood had to be gathered and the fires kept burning. If buns were to be enjoyed for breakfast, then someone had to be up at midnight mixing and baking. Gardens were usually not close to the village houses; houses were generally near the beach while the best fertile soil could well be in higher areas deeper into the jungle. Family members who worked in the gardens would leave before light, sometimes working all day and sleeping there before making their way back the following day. They carried potatoes, bananas and other crops in heavily laden string bags.

Cooks in the villages worked tirelessly before, during, and after all classes. When we held a combined course in the larger towns, it was no easier for the cooks. They had to find a place to prepare, cook and clean. Supplies had to be transported, and there were not the same sources of fresh food as there were in the villages. At one such course in Gizo, I was deeply impressed by the commitment of the women who provided the meals. I knew that some of them would have preferred to attend the courses. They worked so hard day and night, that I wanted to reward them in some way at the conclusion of the week.

I was staying in Paradise Lodge, a rest house that had an amazing view but was an uphill walk of two kilometres from the town. I asked the owner, May, if she would be willing to put on a Saturday lunch for the women who had worked hard all week. I invited all of them to attend. May and I did our best to set up the dining room beautifully with white tablecloths and frangipani and hibiscus flowers decorating the tables. I also managed to get a comb and some perfume for each lady, and I planned to share a devotion after the meal based on Proverbs 16:24, "Pleasant words are like honeycomb, sweetness to the soul and health to the body."

The women arrived at the lodge and sat down on the ground outside. I asked them to come upstairs to where the dining room had been prepared. They moved onto the verandah, but did not come inside. It took a lot of encouragement for them to finally come inside and sit down. But nobody said anything. This took me by surprise; I knew most of these women and how they liked nothing better than to sit and story. The silence was off-putting, so I decided to break the ice by sharing the devotion first. I then invited the ladies to fill up their plates with the delicious food May had prepared. Again, all through the meal there was absolute silence.

By now I was feeling very uncomfortable. Thankfully, after the meal Ruriko stood up to speak.

"Pastor Kay, you are probably wondering why no one is talking," she said. Yes, I thought, I certainly am. "When we saw the room, we thought it was set up for a queen. We didn't think we belonged here. Most of us have never sat on a chair at a table before. We are used to sitting on the ground, so this is all very new for us."

As she sat down, I felt deeply embarrassed. I was again reminded of how little I knew and how much I took for granted.

There were many occasions when I had a glimpse of the resourcefulness of the indigenous people.

During one stay in Munda, on New Georgia Island, I was invited to a small island in the lagoon where some of the first missionaries had stayed before moving onto the mainland. Here I was able to participate in vine fishing. Vines from the jungles were fashioned into large lengths of natural netting. Sap was then collected from a particular tree, and it was mixed with sand to form a natural anaesthetic. This, when sprinkled on the water, rendered the reef fish unconscious. The whole village was involved in the process.

I was excited to jump into the water on the reef at low tide along with the islanders. Some of us formed a large circle holding the net and then walked towards each other to make the circle smaller. Others jumped out of canoes and collected fish as they floated on the surface. In no time at all, the canoes were full of fish and we returned to the beach. Fish were then distributed to each family. Such a productive haul was only possible because they did not overfish any one area. That area would now be left alone for up to two years.

Before rice was introduced into Solomon culture, fish and root vegetables were the staple foods (and in most places still are). As we travelled across the ocean in open canoes, many times the boat driver would notice a stirring in the water and veer off course. Throwing in a line attached to a stick or a bottle, with no bait, would almost always result in a beautiful blue fin or yellow fin tuna being hauled aboard. Breakfast! When our first stay in Mono was extended by a week and we had no supplies, we discovered that the locals would sell us large, freshly caught fish every day. The five of us could enjoy a wonderful meal for less than two Australian dollars.

In the middle of 2010, the pastor from Malasova on the east side of Vella approached me about coming there to teach the theology course. He had missed out on attending this course and needed it in order to become a licenced minister. I had pencilled in for a break but was happy to go. While this was primarily for his benefit, he said that others in his small village might join in.

I prepared ten sets of student notes thinking that would be more than adequate. As I arrived by canoe, I saw people travelling from all directions. Word had spread about the course, and we had over fifty participants. That doubled the size of the village for the weeklong course. Everyone was welcomed and accommodated.

During the course, participants had to present a particular topic to the class using object lessons, drama, or songs, as well as verbal explanations. The whole village, looking through the windows of the church, wanted to see the presentations. At one point, smoke wafting in through one of the windows distracted me. To my delight and surprise, the pastor's wife walked into the building literally carrying a fire. This carefully prepared prop served to powerfully communicate her allotted topic. At the conclusion of all of the presentations there was a palpable presence of the Holy Spirit.

I promptly announced that we would not have lunch. The women of Malasova breathed a collective sigh of relief. Unbeknownst to me, the village had run out of food. Every banana, vegetable and grain of rice had been consumed by the unexpected influx of people. Their relief was short-lived however, as, for some unknown reason, I followed with an announcement that there would be a farewell feast before everyone departed for their homes. Normally I would never have been so bold as to make such a presumptuous announcement, but I was so excited at what we had all experienced during the week that I obviously was not thinking in a rational or culturally appropriate way. Nobody said anything. The participants just set about packing and storying with friends they had made, as they waited for the feast to come later in the afternoon.

Knowing something had to be done, one of the church elders paddled out of the river mouth to the ocean to go fishing. He had no bait, yet every time he threw in his line he immediately pulled in a fish. He repeated this process for an hour and then paddled back to the village with a canoe loaded to the brim with fish. At the same time, one of the visiting ladies went for a walk along the river. It was low tide when she noticed some movement in a puddle left by the outgoing tide. Upon closer inspection, she found a fish, taking up the whole length of the puddle. She picked it up and took it back to the kitchen. This was a huge fish and was not of a variety normally seen in the river. So, we had our feast.

Those people not only knew how to fish but also had faith that fish would be provided. Many times have we heard the adage, "Give a man a fish and you feed him for a day. Teach a man to fish and you feed him for life." Solomon Islanders are experts at fishing. It angers me still that there are those who would have the audacity to go to the Solomons in the expectation of teaching them to fish. These are also spiritual people with over a hundred years' experience of the Gospel working powerfully among them. *White men* going to the Solomons with their Western education and their experience of Christianity will always have much to learn from Melanesian brothers and sisters.

These men and women are gifted fishers of both their natural and spiritual resources.

19

The Power of the Gospel

It was while teaching my initial course in Supezei in January 2007 that Jason Doromolovo first alerted me to two deep issues in Solomons' life. These were: 1. The problem of sorcery in the villages, and 2. confusion about about body, soul and spirit in relation to eternal life. The people are very spiritually aware and there is a deep interest in the afterlife.

I soon saw what he meant. In my travels around the islands, I observed deeply held spiritual beliefs and practices. These included the belief that evil spirits could be responsible for injury, sickness, accidents, rough seas and peculiar weather phenomena. Repeated sickness or death in a village could result in someone's family member being accused of being a sorcerer.

The sharing of the Gospel can have many starting points. For the Jews it is that Jesus is the Christ. For the Gentiles it could be the very existence and nature of God. For many in the west, it can be the need to be loved and accepted. There can also be a deep spiritual need to experience forgiveness, to be released from guilt and to be saved from sin. Assurance of eternal life is another matter of spiritual urgency for many individuals and cultures.

In the Solomons, however, I discovered that the most urgent need was often freedom from the fear of evil forces. Melanesian culture is steeped in an awareness of spiritual life. Freedom from the fear of evil can come through the knowledge that the life, death and resurrection of Jesus have won victory over evil. This knowledge is reinforced by the experience that the name of Jesus is powerful enough to break any curse. The presence of The Holy Spirit in the life of the believer takes on much more significance than I had previously realised.

When Jason told me that the greatest challenge faced by Christians in Choiseul was sorcery, I had no idea what he was talking about. While the practices of cannibalism and headhunting were long gone, fear of the spirit world pervaded. I did not realise that, when there was continued sickness, death or were accidents in a community, someone could be accused of sorcery. I was to witness the great distress caused by these accusations.

Prior knowledge and understanding would have enabled me to take Jason's concerns much more seriously, however, I had very little experience in this area. I had encountered a couple of full force personal spiritual attacks. When it was an impending attack on me, I was able to call on the name of Jesus over and over again. At the time this was all I was capable of doing. When a family in the church where I was pastor, came under attack, I felt out of my depth. I was able to consult Troy, a pastor I held in high regard, and with much prayer and careful sharing, we did experience victory in a powerful way. The family and I spent a day in prayer, fasting and reading Scriptures. We then took the authority Jesus gives us to command evil forces, not only to flee, but also to be bound and prevented from going elsewhere. However, because I was never again faced with this challenge in Australia, the knowledge I gained was placed on the back burner of my mind.

Now witnessing spiritual attacks and hearing of their consequences, helped me begin to understand why the truth of the Holy Spirit is such an imperative for Christian training and ministry. It took me two years to develop a course around The Holy Spirit for the Melanesian context and then to travel to each district to share the course. As I travelled and interacted with the people, I continued to learn, not only of the importance of the spiritual battle, but also of how there can be a mixture of Christian beliefs and animistic practices still present in the twenty-first century.

One such course was held in the small village of Lubao on the island of Vella. This village tripled in size as the participants arrived, and it was obvious to all that their main problem was a lack of fresh water. Fresh water springs had been destroyed during the tsunami of 2007 and now there was only one small tank in the village, and it had not rained for two weeks. The problem wasn't openly discussed but I could tell there was concern, there was also hope because they prayed and believed. We arrived in Lubao to a ceremony re-enacting a traditional warrior *attack* and then a welcome feast. By the end of the feast, it had begun to rain. For the entirety of the course, it rained at night but it was fine during the day. God's abundant provision and protection never ceases to amaze me.

Over my years there, many times it was necessary to pray against evil spirits and curses. On one such occasion I had travelled to Honiara, the capital city, ready to return to Australia. I was exhausted and had booked three nights in a hotel to rest before my journey home. I had not planned any ministry during these three days, and was just looking forward to a time for recuperation. However, Myrah from the Honiara church contacted me. I explained that I was really not up to taking any meetings while I was there, and she said that she understood and had therefore only organised two meetings, one during the day and one at night!

To be honest, I did not have a good attitude as I walked to the daytime meeting. It surprised me how many people had made the effort to come at such short notice. I had been told that one young lady had a particular need for prayer, and despite my negative mindset I felt happy to pray for her.

But I did not have any idea of her actual need. It turned out that the young lady was Nini, someone I had met years previously on the island of Kolombangara. She was in Honiara with her mother, Teva, and was now a mother herself. During the worship service, I listened to Nini's story, and it became clear that, rather than being a medical issue, she was experiencing a spiritual attack. She was stricken with severe abdominal pain and Nina and her mother believed that someone had put a curse on her. As we laid hands on her, anointed her with oil, sang, prayed and commanded demons to flee, Nini began to convulse and cough. She hacked up something disgusting and black out of her body. Nini was instantly set free. We all rejoiced, and once again I was humbled. It was never about my knowledge or power. I would have chosen to stay home that day and lounge by the pool. There is always the danger of putting our own felt needs ahead of God's amazing plans.

I realised afresh that when my fighting spirit feels inadequate to a task, God surpasses my limitations. He did not need me, but how incredible that he chose to involve me in His work.

20
The Baptism Question

Baptism has always been closely linked to Christian faith and mission because of the Great Commission. These are the words given by Jesus to his disciples before His ascension to heaven.

"All authority in heaven and on earth has been given to me. Go therefore and make disciples of all nations, baptizing them in the name of the Father and of the Son and of the Holy Spirit, and teaching them to obey everything I have commanded you. And remember, I am with you always, to the end of the age."[16]

Ten days after Jesus' ascension, Peter, filled with the Holy Spirit, addressed the crowd at Pentecost and the crowd responded with the question, "What must we do to be saved?"

"Repent, and be baptized every one of you in the name of Jesus Christ so that your sins may be forgiven; and you will receive the gift of the Holy Spirit."[17]

Since then, throughout church history, baptisms have been carried out using various methods and at various times of a person's life.

John Wesley went as a missionary to Georgia in the American colonies in February 1736. He records in his journal part of a conversation he had with Tomo Chachi, a member of a local native Indian tribe. Tomo Chachi's words contain a warning not to baptise too quickly.

"I am glad you are come. When I was in England, I desired that some would speak the great Word to me and my nation then desired to hear it; but now we are all in confusion. Yet I am glad you are come. I will go up and speak to the wise men of our nation; and I hope they will hear. But we would not be made Christians as the Spaniards make Christians: we would be taught, before we are baptized."[18]

At that first course I held in Supezei in January 2007, the topic of believer's baptism was discussed at length. It became clear that this was a sensitive issue. When John Goldic came as a Wesleyan Methodist missionary to the Solomons in 1902, he did not perform any baptisms for the first five years. Then a memorable event occurred.

It was in about the sixth year of mission work at Roviana that Mr and Mrs Goldie were awakened about midnight on Easter Sunday. All the boys on the station, about fifty of them, were gathered outside the house at Kokengolo. They stated that they could not sleep; they wanted to know if the preaching was true.

"Did 'Karisto' (Christ), God's only Son, die for us, and rise again?" They had been wanting to follow Him for months but did not know the way. When Mr Goldie heard this, his heart was filled with an unspeakable joy. The depression vanished, and he regretted the moments in which he had almost given up in despair.

The boys were put "on trial" for twelve months, and then baptised. Mr Rooney came from Choiseul for the occasion and shared in the service. There were many baptismal services in later years, and many bigger, but none meant so much to the missionaries as that first service when forty-eight young converts stood before a great assembly of natives and were baptised.[19]

Goldie did not rush believers into baptism but spent time teaching and discipling them. Throughout the rest of his fifty-year ministry in the Solomons, the only recorded baptisms were of believers who had come to faith.

At some point after Goldie's departure, however, infant baptism replaced believer's baptism. The strongly held belief grew that if you were baptised as a baby, you were saved and were going to heaven. Whichever branch of Christianity you were baptised into, there you stayed faithfully until you died. This did not mean that you necessarily attended church or had any signs of an active faith. It was the faith of the parents in presenting their child for baptism that was being honoured.

Because of my conversations with Ray and Gwen, I was aware of this strongly held tenet and I was careful in that first Supezci course not to insist on believer's baptism. The fact that eleven students came forward at the end and asked to be baptised, displayed their conviction. I will never forget the sight of those adults running into the water to be baptised. The beautiful sandy beach of Supezei was a perfect location for this emotional occasion.

My own experience with baptism was somewhat chequered. My three brothers and I were baptised as infants, into the Anglican Church (Church of England) because my father had been baptised an Anglican, though ironically none of the family ever attended an Anglican church. Then when my daughter Dimity was born, I wanted her to be baptised. I certainly was not a Christian at the time although I was praying every day for God to help me get through the next twenty-four hours. Deep inside me was a conviction that I wanted to do everything I could for my daughter, and for some reason that included baptism.

I went to see the Uniting Church minister in my nearest town. He was very welcoming and supportive. However, rather than have all my friends and relatives travel two hours for the occasion, I decided to move the baptism to Logan City, where it would be convenient for everyone to attend. My friendly local minister gave me the name of the Logan Uniting Church minister. Meeting him was a very different experience. He was not warm and certainly not welcoming. I felt he was judgmental, critical and condemnatory. "Why should I baptise your baby since you are not married?" he asked. At no point did he offer me any insight into Christianity or even into what baptism meant. He reluctantly agreed, simply because I would not back down from my request. I was all fired up and I didn't want my daughter missing out on anything because of my actions and choices.

The baptism went ahead, and Dimity wore the same dress I had worn for my baptism as an infant. It was a great family occasion, but I remember being so stressed by the way I had been treated, that I backed my car into a tree as I left the church grounds.

When I finally came to faith in Jesus, my new understanding of baptism led me to want the world to know that my life belonged to Him, so I decided to be baptised as a believer. I knew the joy of those people in Supezei because I had experienced it then. Five years later, in one of the highlights of my pastoral life, my mum asked me to baptise her. She was baptised in her backyard pool, as were many others from the Woodridge church in the five years I was there. This included George who by now was in his eighties, and Mum's friend, Colleen.

People from as far away as Honiara heard about the baptisms in Supezei, and the general reaction was one of great concern. Aware that baptism was a sensitive topic, I continued to be careful never to push the issue as their teacher.

During my next trip to Maravari on Vella la Vella in 2008, I was asked to baptise some babies as many many babies in the community had never been baptised. I agreed because that was their expected practice. The pastor from the nearby village of Kenepide, heard about this proposal and asked if his congregation could join us for this special service. Everyone was excited.

Or so I thought.

In most villages there is a house set aside for visitors. I was descending the stairs of the rest house to go to church when the District Superintendent met me. "Some of these mothers are not married and their babies should not be baptised," he said. Totally surprised, I responded that they were already in the church, and I had already met with them. I knew that they would be dressed in white and prepared for their babies' baptisms. Cancellation at this late stage did not seem feasible.

I walked into the church and sat down before being overcome by what had just happened. Tears streamed down my face. Here was I, remembering how I had been treated as a single mother wanting her child baptised, about to baptise babies that a church leader thought were unworthy because their mothers were not married. I was overcome by the grace of God. I was thinking to myself: could it be that God chose me to intervene on behalf of these single mothers? I took each child into my arms, baptised them and prayed for them. I recall this as a privilege too huge to be measured.

Over time, believer's baptism became accepted and desired. Babies were dedicated to God, officially named and welcomed into the church family, whereas adults who had been churchgoers now wanted to present themselves for believer's baptism. There was an eagerness to testify publicly to their faith in Jesus.

Wherever baptisms were held, the ocean or river was beautifully prepared by placing flowers floating on bamboo sticks around the area. Candidates testified with much singing and rejoicing. On one occasion in Malasova, on the western side of Vella, there was a heavy tropical downpour at the very time the baptisms were scheduled. Such rain usually went on for hours, so I was asked if we should postpone the baptisms. The noise on the tin roof of the church was so loud that hearing testimonies was impossible. Then suddenly, the rain stopped. Every candidate gave his or her testimony. We walked to the river and carried out every baptism. After the last person reached the riverbank, the rain recommenced and went on again for many more hours.

There continue to be requests for believer's baptisms. Recently, in 2022, eighty youth came forward to be baptised during a youth convention at Maravari. On every occasion of baptism that I witnessed, the desire to be baptised came to the believer as a result of something significant happening in their life. Either they had experienced a fresh realisation of what Jesus had done for them personally, or there was a deep desire to live a Christian life and to not just be identified as a Christian.

21
Equipping Teachers

During my seven years of itinerant teaching in the Solomons, I met some remarkable people who still live in my heart. What follows are stories of but a few.

After those first combined courses in Supezei in January 2007, word spread to the other Wesleyan districts. There was great excitement and anticipation about the second course, to be held in July that year at Maravari on the island of Vella la Vella. I organised a team from Australia to come and help with tutoring during the course. A canoe-load of participants arrived from the New Georgia District and Jason Doromolovo brought a large delegation from Choiseul. The most exciting thing was seeing the sweet reunions between those who had met at Supezei six months earlier and had formed strong bonds.

One participant who came was Nakalo from the island of Ranongga. He was the young man who had spent a year working in the jungle to prepare for the youth convention in 2004. He had also been at Supezei. I wondered why he always sat at the back of the room and did not appear to participate. He explained that he only had two years of schooling and could not read or write well. Apart from not having liked school, he was the youngest in his family, which meant there was a degree of responsibility for him to stay home and help in practical ways, including looking after the elderly.

This realisation prompted me to contact Elizabeth, a long-time friend and special education teacher. I asked if she would come and spend two weeks with Nakalo as his private tutor. I have never seen anybody learn as quickly as he did. He was thriving. He was soon reading the Bible more fluently than his peers. Over the next few years, he would come to the same courses two or three times until he felt he understood. More importantly, he wanted to feel confident that he could go back to Ranongga and teach his own people.

Nakalo went on to be one of the first students to become a licenced minister and later an ordained minister. Since 2007 he has married and had four daughters and a son. Now that some of his children are at primary school, Nakalo has also set about completing the primary school education he missed out on. His learning places him in a position where he has no need to do this, but such is his integrity that he wants to complete all levels of primary school and then complete secondary school. He is now a District Superintendent and a wonderful example of a committed, godly leader to his people.

The group that travelled from New Georgia included Watson Otota and his wife, Ruriko. Watson was the son of Helen, whom I met on my first trip to Gizo in 2002 but who had since passed away. Watson had for many years led a life away from God and had the accompanying reputation. He worked for Solomon Airlines and travelled on flights overseas, where he succumbed to many temptations. He and Ruriko had had a daughter but were then estranged, mainly because of his drinking and infidelity. Watson fathered several children with other women during his years away from Ruriko, though he did take responsibility for the upbringing of each child.

After his mother's funeral, Watson made a promise that he would come back to God and build a church in her village. Helen, you may remember as the woman who, in 2002 walked many hours to Gizo, learning the details of the previous night's sermon on her way. After twelve years apart, he asked Ruriko to take him back. She agreed, but only after he promised to give up drinking. She also welcomed his children and became their mother. Their first daughter was now a mother herself, and they soon had a second daughter of their own, making it a large family. Now they had come together to Maravari, to participate in courses in Evangelism and the New Testament.

Watson was initially offended by some of the concepts he encountered and argued sharply with Ruriko. There were also late night debates with other students. It is a teacher's dream to have students debating issues and considering issues for themselves. The result was that Watson became more attentive in class and asked searching questions. By the end of the training, he was a changed man. His heart was set on fire, and he began to speak to everyone he met about Jesus. He was a natural evangelist and his impact on people outside of the church was profound because they could observe his transformed life.

After Maravari, both Watson and Ruriko continued with their studies and became ordained ministers. They transformed their village; building the church he had dreamed of to honour his mother and making an ongoing difference in their community.

Eventually Watson became District Superintendent for the Central West District, but unfortunately he died suddenly of a heart attack soon after Christmas 2020. He left a huge gap in many lives, but his example of loving people into the Kingdom of God will never be forgotten.

Teaching the series of courses in Maravari gave me many more opportunities to learn about the culture. I learned, for example, the importance of communicating with the chief of the host village to ask permission to hold training there.

Because of a tragic death in the village during a course, I also began to learn the importance of honouring cultural practices after a death. We paused our courses until the funeral was over. The family had to make the coffin and dig the hole for the burial. The deceased person lay in their house, and mourners, towels draped over their shoulders in order to wipe up tears, would visit day and night. The women began wailing well before they reached the house and this continued throughout the night. Services were held inside the house every morning and night, until the burial. The burial had to take place as soon as possible because of the environmental conditions. Ten days of mourning followed the funeral and then there was a feast, after which mourners returned to their homes. I was told that another feast would follow one hundred days later, to mark the end of the family's mourning period. I later discovered that each tribe had its own specific customs, but my main lesson on that first occasion was that when a death occurred everything stopped, and for everyone the priority is to minister to the grieving family.

The evangelism course had students working together in their language groupings. I worked with those from Vella, who spoke the Bilua language. At the conclusion of the course, the groups went to different villages to present what they had learnt. I stayed in Maravari with the Bilua group.

We were welcomed into a leaf house where there were a dozen adults in one room and thirty children in another.

The group of students from Vella presented the Gospel and performed dramas in their own language. At the conclusion, the students asked the hosts if they would like to accept the free gift of eternal life that Jesus offered. There was silence.

After what I thought was an adequate pause, I stood up and thanked the head of the house for allowing us to visit and proceeded to leave, expecting the group to follow me. Just before I reached the door, I heard a small voice. "Reverend Kay, you have come here today to offer us the free gift of eternal life and we would like to accept it."

I was so stunned that I quite inappropriately replied, "What, all of you?" I did not understand that no one would speak until the head of the house had spoken. When he did speak, he spoke for everyone. I was reminded of those events in the New Testament where we read of whole households coming to faith. I was humbled to see this take place before my eyes. The Vella students were able to carry out follow-up visits with everyone from this household and others who joined them.

The students were extremely diligent. The courses of study were intensive, with six hours of classes, five days a week. They stayed up through the night, with the only light coming from torches as they completed their assignments. The standard of work was exceptional, all the more so when you consider that fewer than ten per cent of the students had gone past primary school.

At the conclusion of the two 2007 combined courses, it was evident that there were gifted teachers and leaders among the participants. Since secondary schooling was not free and was only available to a limited number who had excelled in primary school, most of our students had missed out on this opportunity. One man, Peter Anama, had always done well in primary school and had expected to go on to secondary school. However, when the final results and rankings came out, he was placed lower than students with a poorer academic record. It made no sense, but he had failed to make the cut and could not go on to secondary school. There was nothing he could do.

At the conclusion of our time in Maravari, Peter stood up to testify that God does not have limits. He was so excited because God did not exclude anyone. He testified powerfully about how all could not only enter the Kingdom of God through faith, but also excel as the Holy Spirit enabled them. He was a natural teacher.

Another very gifted man was Richard Solomon Soto, the brother of Nakalo from Ranongga. He had some post-secondary education and would later be selected to attend the Christian Leaders' Training College in Mount Hagen, Papua New Guinea. He is now ordained and is assistant principal of the Solomon Island Wesleyan Methodist Bible College.

Back in 1988, when I declared to God that I would go anywhere in the world, his call was to "preach the Gospel to the poor". I was so excited about this "call to missions" that I did not stop to analyse exactly what it meant. I just got on with sharing the good news of Jesus Christ in many forms in a variety of circumstances.

During my time as evangelist for the South Queensland Wesleyan district, for example, I observed that ninety per cent of the Christians I had met never intentionally shared their faith. I called upon many resources to equip individuals to engage in conversations about the Gospel, including 'Christianity Explained', 'Train to Proclaim', 'Evangelism Explosion', 'Contagious Christianity' and the Alpha course. Each of these courses proved to be valuable and had a lasting impact on the participants.

Another resource was the Kids' Evangelism Explosion program, developed largely by Virginia Woodward, a member of Fig Tree Anglican Church in New South Wales.

Kids' EE provided a method of presenting the Gospel using interactive methods. Scriptures were learnt using physical activities and games, and the content was all presented using drama and song. This is ideally suited to the Melanesian context. Virginia travelled to the Solomons, accompanied by Kerri Burton, to help kick start the program. The plan was to carry out the training in local Wesleyan churches in all districts, however, for this to happen on an ongoing basis, there had to be locally trained teachers.

I realised it was essential to understand how best to communicate the Gospel in Solomon Islands cultural context, and how to equip nationals to share their faith with their own people. I came to the strong belief that this was to be my ongoing mission.

Two amazing women, Sarota from New Georgia and Paulyn from the village of Malasova on Vella, also stood out as gifted and natural teachers. Later they would both travel with me taking more and more of an active role. Later still, Ruriko joined them as did June, a student who had done an amazing job of teaching in her own church and local community. As a matter of fact, when June completed the Kids EE program in her village, the local primary school principal closed the school for the day so everyone could attend the final presentations. The principal testified as to how much the children's behaviour had improved since they participated in Kids EE.

The fact that the students' evaluations often took the form of oral presentations meant that identifying such gifts was easier. Most participants were comfortable performing songs and drama, so it was not too big a stretch to give an oral presentation, unlike students in the west who almost exclusively, complete written exams.

Not all students felt comfortable in front of the class however. I remember the first time Gutilyn, a young single mother from Ranongga, attended a course in Gizo. She left the day before presentations were due. She did not feel adequate to stand in front of the class. I do not know what changed for her, but the following year, she came back to complete that subject and went on to complete many others. She married another student, Eddie, a pastor on Vella, and they ministered wonderfully together.

For most of the students, English was, at best, their fourth language. I knew it was imperative that I learn to speak Pijin as quickly as possible. It was also essential to use creative teaching methods such as drama, physical games and activities, art, craft and music.

From the beginning my plan was to train indigenous men and women to become the teachers. The membership course contained Wesleyan theology, history and articles of religion. It was taught in as many locations as possible so that people could understand what it meant to be part of the Wesleyan Methodist Church and decide if that was where they and their families belonged. A parallel purpose was to equip the pastors to teach this course themselves so they could bring their own people into membership. Once pastors had completed the membership course twice, they could then teach it in the villages on their own islands.

It took time to supersede the adopted concept that only ordained ministers had the authority to minister. All believers have the same Holy Spirit. There was no need to wait for a visiting ordained minister or someone from overseas to experience the life changing work of the Holy Spirit. Each believer could pray for healing. Local pastors could baptise their own people and bring them into membership. Licenced ministers could perform weddings and funerals. They were equipped and free to minister to their own people in their own languages. It was an exciting time.

Sarota was the first to travel with me and to start formal training as a teacher. She and her husband desperately wanted to have children, but she had been told she could not have children and was actually scheduled to have a hysterectomy. As we travelled together, she shared how she would love to have a baby. She said she would love to sing to her child while he or she was in her womb. Through our tears we prayed. We also believed. Sarota did not have the surgery, and she and her husband now have two boys. Her teacher training was cut short, but she has built a church in her own village and is now the Wesleyan Church's National Director of Children. She uses her gifts daily to influence others.

Paulyn and Ruriko, who also travelled with me, have both gone on to train others. There was a time when they would be teaching a class and would look at me to check for my approval. I soon realised that not only was I not needed, but that my presence was in fact, detrimental to their progress. Subsequently, in 2012, when we were planning a combined course at the village of Soncke in Choiseul District, we organised for June, Ruriko and Paulyn to take the whole Kids' EE program by themselves. I would teach the combined course called Inductive Bible Study for the adults during the first week but would not attend the Kids' EE training.

Much time was spent in planning who would be responsible for each lesson and who for the resources required. The ladies were nervous but also excited and there was a great sense of anticipation from everyone.

Unfortunately, things did not go as planned.

Towards the end of my course, I began to suffer from intense head pain. Describing it as a headache does not adequately convey the intensity. I can only describe it as feeling, that in order to move, I needed to sever my head from my body and carry it around separately.

As I became more and more immobile, June suggested that I take a malaria test. I had no fever or other common malaria symptoms, but I was told that sometimes malaria could strike like this. I took the test and struggled to lie back on my mat. A runner came to inform the leaders that my test was positive and that it was "XXXX". I didn't understand what that meant, but I knew that my condition was deteriorating.

Unable to take the common anti-malarial medication Doxycycline, because I was allergic to it, I carried Chloroquine with me and so was able to take that as prescribed. But it was obvious to all that I needed to get to hospital. Thankfully, the boat we had chartered was returning to Gizo to take home those students who were not participating in the Kids' EE program. Ahead of me was the prospect of a voyage that would take at least four hours if it were a fine sea. There would be no quick respite.

While waiting for transport, I asked Paulyn, June and Ruriko to come to my room. They were nervous, as I was obviously not going to be in the village during their course. I reassured them that I felt it was God's plan. They didn't need me, and if I was close by, they may call on me when they didn't need to. I said I was excited they had this opportunity all on their own and was extremely confident in their abilities.

Before we had finished praying, the District Superintendent for Choiseul knocked on the door. He had been away in Australia for four years studying in a Bible college. Everyone had been excited to have him back and had appointed him as their district leader. He told us he had cancelled the Kids' EE course.

We were all in shock. "Why?" I pleaded.

"Because you won't be here."

I explained that I was not going to be a part of the course anyway.

He responded, "What if someone asks a question that the ladies cannot answer?"

"Well, you will be there to answer," I replied.

His mind was made up, however. "We only value Western education," he said.

This exchange left me feeling worse than the malaria. As he left, we collapsed into each other's arms, crying. "What am I doing here if they're not going to accept their own national teachers?" I wondered. It was the last rational thought I had for a long time.

I had to be carried down to the beach to get on the boat. I hardly knew the captain, but I realised I was losing my mind when I greeted him with an enthusiastic, "Hi, babe!" I was put under the half-cabin for protection from the sun on the trip to Gizo. However, it wasn't long into the journey that I was completely overcome with heat, from being in that confined space with no fresh air. I knew I had to cool down, and I knew that water would cool me down. I proceeded to crawl out from the cabin, ready to jump overboard. The men didn't move. Either they were in shock or they were just reluctant to grab me. Thankfully the women pulled me back. I fought them with whatever strength I had, but of course they succeeded in saving me from myself.

At that point, Russell Kaide, the District Superintendent of New Georgia, stood up in the rear of the boat. That in itself was not a good idea. He proceeded to pray in his own language. As he prayed, I felt something tangible move from my head, down through my body and right to my feet. I wasn't instantly healed, but I believe that in that moment, God preserved my life.

The three women held me for the rest of the journey. I felt them rise up and lift me together as we navigated the swells, saving me from the impact of the bumps and thumps. Some months later when I met the boat captain back in Gizo, and addressed him appropriately, he told me that I was unconscious for most of the trip and that everyone was extremely worried about me. "Once you are unconscious it is usually the end," he said.

By the grace of God, I made it to Gizo hospital. No beds were available in the wards, so I was placed on a trolley in the emergency room. Like the 'hi babe', there were more inappropriate comments but this time to the doctor who came to examine me. It was as if I was outside of myself observing the behaviour of a different person. I was in such a confused state of mind and so physically weak that the only thing that gave me comfort was the singing of the women who had accompanied me to hospital.

For several days I was never alone. Gloria came to join Paulyn, Ruriko and June. Two women were always at my bedside, while the other two slept outside on wooden benches. I was not aware at the time, but four of the men also took shifts to be security for the women. In the mornings, the whole team gathered around the trolley and held morning devotions. I was being lovingly ministered to by those whom I had come to minister.

During the first night I heard some horrific sounds coming from a patient entering the emergency room. The sounds were so awful that my first thought was that the patient must be a child who was possessed. No more trolleys were available, so the patient was placed on the floor. The ladies who had been attending to me, now turned to help this patient and her mother. I soon learned from the conversations, that the patient was a young woman with a small baby. I was thinking she was mentally ill and was horrified when considering how she could have conceived a child.

However, I soon found out she was suffering the same strain of malaria that I was enduring. I began to realise: there but for the grace of God go I. Mental illness or death is often the outcome of this illness.

I knew God had preserved my life on that canoe trip, but months later, still recovering I became increasingly upset by what had happened when the course was cancelled. I wrote to all of the District Superintendents seeking their thoughts on the course of training and on their willingness to accept national teachers in the future. They all strongly affirmed the strategy of training nationals to be teachers and their support for those who had already been trained.

I am not privy to conversations they had among themselves and the stories that were told. I do know that a year or so later, the Choiseul District Superintendent invited the three women back to Choiseul to run the Kids' EE training. He was so impressed with their teaching and the quality of their presentations that he fully supported their on-going ministry.

My students ministered to me so beautifully and in so many ways, that my faith in their abilities and their future was soundly reinforced. I could see myself stepping away as their teacher, confident that they would flourish.

22
The Need to Endorse

At the very beginning, my goal had been education, empowerment and endorsement. Over time I had come to dislike the term empowerment because it signified to me that one group of people saw themselves as having power, and when they deemed that another group was worthy enough, they would give them some of that power. My priority instead became the endorsement of the qualities, abilities and giftedness of the national Christians and their ministries.

Within the first year, I was able to recognise the giftedness of people with whom I was working. Hall, Dorah, Gloria and Ruriko exemplified grace, mercy and sacrificial service. Jason displayed amazing leadership; Watson and John had natural gifts of evangelism; Soto, Nakalo, Paulyn, Sarota, June, Ambrose and Horton were gifted teachers. Thankfully, the Choiseul incident served to elevate the national trainers, but it also illustrated to me the importance of having an exit strategy.

On many occasions teachers and teams had come from Australia to assist with courses. That was necessary in the early years. Now that there were qualified nationals, I firmly believed the best assistants were the Solomon Islanders themselves. They had completed the courses, knew the culture and each spoke several Solomons languages.

During my time in the Solomons, I was delighted to travel twice to Papua New Guinea to visit Melanesian training centres. One such visit was in 2011 when I spent time at a Bible college in the Western Highlands. I stayed with an American missionary couple. They had been there for twenty years and were preparing to leave the field. They were seriously considering closing the college because they could not attract any missionaries from the United States to replace them. I was flabbergasted. Where were the national Christians who they had trained over their twenty-year-stay? They did all the administration, teaching and library work themselves. It was unthinkable to me that no one had been trained in any of these tasks and no one had been endorsed to carry on the work.

I was invited to speak at the evening chapel service. As I walked into the room, I saw that women were sitting on the stools on the right side of the room, and the men on the left. That felt familiar; it was the same in Solomon Islands. Feeling at home, I sat with the women. It was only when I went to the front to speak that I saw three chairs next to each other at the back of the room. The missionary couple were sitting in two and the third was empty. Obviously, that was where it was assumed I would sit. My heart broke a little.

During another visit in 2012, I attended a meeting between American, Australian and Papua New Guinean leaders to discuss the future direction of theological training. I sat through the morning listening to the perspectives of the Westerners. At morning tea, I asked the national leaders, "Why haven't you said anything?

This is your college and your people's future. What do you think?" The reply broke my heart a little further, "These men are our bosses. We don't want to say anything in case we say the wrong thing."

I came away from that visit with two thoughts. Firstly, how did that happen? Secondly, it must never happen in Solomon Islands. As I saw it, the role of mission-sending organisations was to raise the focus on missions within their churches, encourage those called to mission and support their missionaries before, during and after their term on the mission field. I had never seen missionaries or their sending organisations as the "bosses". In my frame of reference, missionaries were to be servants and to serve the needs decided upon by national leaders in other cultures. In the nineteenth century, when there were no national leaders, missionaries led the churches and made the decisions. However, surely this was only ever intended to be a temporary circumstance.

After these experiences I was more determined than ever to do all I could in my sphere of influence to encourage Solomon Islanders not to rely on Westerners setting their course and steering their ship. After deep thought I realised that there was a need for resources and practical assistance to make this happen. The challenge was how to provide these without taking ownership and control. Underlying that was a very specific challenge. How can we resist the practice to "Westernise" the people and the practices of the church? It is extremely likely that Melanesian tribal communities more closely resemble biblical Christianity than individualist, consumerist Western society.

It was heartening to see Curtis Williams, a young man from the USA go to the Bible College in PNG to stand in the gap. His work and influence was significant. After that time, Don and Cheri Floyd, faithful, long-term missionaries, returned to PNG to work with the indigenous national leaders. Together, they have ensured the ongoing value and relevance of their Bible College. This now indigenous-run Bible College is an encouraging example to other Melanesian churches of how missionaries can successfully work towards the training and endorsement of indigenous leaders.

The first inkling that I should leave the Solomons came after that experience in Choiseul when I was told by the District Superintendent, "We only value Western training." His comment had made me question my whole philosophy of training national believers during the years I had been there.

In June 2012, I flew back to Australia for the birth of my first grandchild, Indiana Kay. Being a grandmother brings me indescribable joy. For the next three months I was able to combine my home missions work of visiting churches with the delights of this newfound role.

Before Indiana's birth, Dimity asked me, "What do you want to be called, Mum? Grandma, Nanna or some other variation?"

My first response was that I had no strong preference. However, as I thought about the options, one word kept coming to me: Zai. This was the word for grandmother in the Babatana language of Choiseul. I heard it so often while staying with Hall and Dorah and their grandchildren that it seemed a natural choice in respectful acknowledgement of a culture I had loved and appreciated for twenty years.

When I returned to the Solomons and shared the stories of my granddaughter and the choice of Zai as my new name, there was much rejoicing. I soon learned that Zai trumped Reverend. To be a grandmother was such an important role in their communities. It was a title of respect. I was now called "Zai Kay" instead of "Reverend Kay", and that name change became a significant impetus in transitioning out of ministry in Solomon Islands.

The irony was that, as much as I felt like I belonged, I knew even more strongly that my time must end in order for the national leaders, teachers and pastors to flourish without my influence. As more and more students completed their studies to become licenced and ordained ministers, my leaving would be an expression of trust in them.

My final transition out of my role in Solomon Islands came at the National Conference in January 2014. All subjects required for ordination had been made available and seven candidates were presented for ordination, along with several others who were acknowledged as licensed ministers. Land had been secured at Noro, in the New Georgia District, to establish a national headquarters and a centralised training centre. I was not able to visit all the local churches before my departure, but I was at least able to visit each one of the five districts. These farewells were heartfelt occasions that will stay with me for the rest of my life.

I don't think I was born a teacher, but my surroundings and the influences on my life led me into a field that suited me. My father was a teacher, an explorer and an amateur inventor. He lit the flame of my desire to know how things worked. My inquisitive mind and thirst for knowledge first led me to want to understand and then to pass on that understanding to others who would continue to pass the baton.

Part Three
The Indwelling Spirit

I came that they may have life, and have it abundantly. I am the good shepherd. The good shepherd lays down his life for the sheep.

John 10:10–11 (NRSV)

If the Spirit of him who raised Jesus from the dead dwells in you, he who raised Christ from the dead will give life to your mortal bodies also through his Spirit that dwells in you.

Romans 8:11 (NRSV)

23

Tupelo Honey

The best word to describe how I felt when I did return to Australia permanently after seven years involved in the mission is "depleted." I was still recovering from the cerebral malaria; I had also endured Ross River Fever and was battling with an ongoing skin infection. This infection started on my chest and, became increasingly severe, spreading over my abdomen and into my groin.

Although I had managed to see two different doctors in Solomon Islands, I had not been able to get any relief. It was only when I returned to Australia and had swabs taken, that I received a correct diagnosis and treatment. Because this infection had been in my system for several years it took a long time to be completely eradicated. My immunity was low, and I had three bouts of pneumonia in my first year of return.

Lacking in energy and strength, my rural property was the best place for my recovery to start. By the grace of God, faithful tenants and low council rates, I had kept the property in the Sunshine Coast Hinterland that I had purchased from Adrian forty years earlier. This was where

I had lived in a shed when I was pregnant and where I desperately called out to God on a daily basis during my pregnancy and after the birth of Dimity. When Dimity was born, I decided to name the property after a Van Morrison song called, 'Tupelo Honey.' It seemed like this song captured my feelings of love for Dimity.

I had since built a house and sub-divided the land, selling off five acres. The money it raised allowed me to study and to minister. For most of the past twenty-five years, the house had been rented out, but it had always been my intention to retire there and work hard to establish a beautiful property.

When Tupelo Honey was rented out, the many tenants had looked after the house but neglected the property, some even damaging it in one way or another. I was faced with six acres of undulating land covered in noxious lantana and rat's tail grass, together with old car bodies and car parts strewn throughout the gullies. It was almost impossible to get rid of the rat's tail when the adjoining unmanaged properties were covered in it. It was easiest, although labour intensive, to get rid of the lantana by digging and pulling out the extensive root system of each plant. Some days I only managed to dig one complex patch of lantana, but little by little I established victory over this invasive plant. With the help of "Lucy", my wonderful four-wheel-drive mower, I conquered every slope.

After establishing gardens along the long driveway, planting many trees, building a playground for my growing number of grandchildren and creating tropical gardens around the house, I was gradually able to enjoy my own piece of paradise. It was after two years of hard work, during one morning's mowing, I paused to survey my property from its highest point. "This place looks the best it ever has," I thought.

After my shower and an enjoyable lunch, I sat down to

relax and watch a movie. I did not get as far as turning on the television. Suddenly I was hit with an incredible pain in the middle of my chest.

It knocked me to the floor but thankfully I had put my phone on charge right next to where I fell and I was able to dial Triple Zero. I could barely move, but I did manage to put myself into the recovery position. The paramedics later told me it took them twenty-three minutes to get there but the events from then on are very hazy. I know they gave me an injection and an ECG. They also rang the Sunshine Coast University Hospital and arranged for a doctor to meet us on the Bruce Highway part way through the one-hour trip.

By the time they put me into the back of the ambulance, I had enough capacity to ring my daughter. I told her I was in an ambulance and going to hospital with chest pain. She offered to come up immediately. Dimity now had four children and lived over two hours away. I think I was as high as a kite from whatever drugs they gave me when I said, "No. Don't worry about that, wait and see what happens." With the phone on speaker, one of the paramedics said, "Tell her to come up immediately." The last thing I remember in that vehicle was that same paramedic telling me he was just going to cut off my shirt so he could put on the defibrillator pads. My next recollection is of being wheeled into theatre where a team of people in scrubs and masks were waiting to work on me.

I had no warning symptoms or any inkling that I could be a candidate for a heart attack. As a matter of fact, I was the fittest I had been in a long, long time. As well as the physical work on the property, I was boxercising three times a week and riding my bike at least sixty kilometres a week.

It was only at my follow-up hospital visit six months later that my cardiologist was able to give me the explanation of what happened. He showed me a ten-year-time-lapse video of the inside of a coronary artery and what happens with the build-up of cholesterol. It looked like a geographical profile of peaks and valleys. Although my cholesterol was not high, a "peak" had broken off and was floating in my coronary artery. My own platelets had swung into action, identifying this as a foreign body. The platelets now surrounding the offending piece of cholesterol were my own body's defence system and they formed a one hundred per cent blockage in my coronary artery.

It was by the grace of God that I survived. I had only just switched phone providers because my previous provider gave me no coverage inside the house. My phone had been within my reach and had a strong signal. The two paramedics and their vehicle were in the nearest town and able to render immediate assistance. The doctor was available to be picked up on the way to the hospital. Amazing advances in treatment for heart attack patients meant that I received the best possible care, where in previous years, survival would have been unlikely.

I was affected emotionally as well as physically by my heart attack. However, I was determined to fight back and threw myself into cardiac rehab. Walking five minutes, twice a day grew week by week until I was walking for an hour. My church, the Mary Valley Wesleyan, held a working bee on my property during which any as-yet-uncleared land was finally cleared. The love and practical support I received from my church family was phenomenal.

Having a heart attack was a turning point for me. It became an easy decision to sell the property. I did not feel I could maintain the physical effort necessary to keep it looking so good. More importantly, while isolation and distance from my family were factors that had not previously caused me concern, they now did. I knew it was time for a change.

In some ways Tupelo Honey was part of my identity. I recalled with fondness, the day so many years earlier when I first saw the block and loved it. I remembered falling in love with the man who sold it to me on that same day. I reminisced about camping out with friends and planting one hundred trees. This was the place I went to when I was pregnant and my relationship ended. After walking out on Adrian with nothing, here was where I lived in the shed and experienced violent morning sickness with only my dog, Magic, for company. It was here I experienced motherhood. I treasured every memory.

I had tried to sell the property several times over the years, when money was tight. Once a scheduled auction had been accompanied by a torrential Queensland storm and nobody had come. Another time the sale fell through on the day of settlement, and I spent a day crying. I recall when I was in Bible college and presented myself to God as willing to go anywhere in the world, I had sketched houses I might like to live in one day. After drawing one design with surrounding gardens, I suddenly realised this was the place I already had. There was no other "dream house" for me this side of heaven.

God had kept the property for me. It had been my haven, the place where I could live out my dreams. Now that it was everything I had ever hoped it would be, it was time to leave. I still miss it, but I knew that God's timing was perfect. Had I stayed there during Covid-19 and the lockdowns, I would not have been able to travel to visit my family.

I was also able to have precious years with my mother, Audrey, before she passed away. Mum celebrated her ninetieth birthday with all her children, grandchildren and great-grandchildren. Not long after this wonderful celebration, her failing heart meant she could no longer stay in her own home. She moved into a Woodridge nursing home just five minutes from the house she had lived in for sixty-five years and where she already knew some other long time Woodridge residents. It was the same familiar bushland which formed the backdrop for her new place of living. Mum's last years were marked by humility and grace. She never complained and right up until the end, put the needs of others above her own. Mum would always start our prayer time by praying for others. My brothers and I all enjoyed playing cards with her until a few weeks before her death. It was such a special honour to talk with Mum about heaven and to pray with her.

24

The Power of Forgiveness

In my mind, leaving Tupelo Honey was also severing a tie I had with Adrian. I had resented him for many years and at many times had been filled with anger toward him. There was a time when I was so angry that I would look at funeral notices and be disappointed that his name was not there.

There were three factors that could have resulted in my being consumed by this rage.

The first was his treatment of me. My anger about this subsided when I realised that his only crime was in not loving me, as I wanted him to. He could have been kinder. He could have been more honest. But as an adult it was my choice to stay with him in, what was, an unhealthy relationship.

The second factor was actually anger at myself. How could I have been so stupid? Why didn't I listen to my friends? Why didn't I accept as a huge alarm bell that he wanted nothing to do with my family? Loving him was certainly unhealthy and all consuming, but it was my own actions and choices that I regretted most.

It took some years of walking with Jesus before I was finally able to forgive myself. An early thought that I had when I did begin this journey with Jesus was: Why didn't this happen ten years ago and save me all this heartache? Now, for several reasons, I am thankful for those years in the wilderness. Those years made me stronger and brought me to a point where I knew, in the future, I would never allow any man to dominate me and lead me in wrong directions. These were the years that taught me to take responsibility for my own choices and their consequences. They also took out of my life any judgmental attitudes I may have otherwise had towards people who lived differently. By the grace, mercy and love shown to me, I was able to love others regardless of their circumstances and lifestyles.

A more difficult thing to forgive was Adrian's neglect of his own daughter. This was the third factor that contributed to my anger. I could cope with whatever he did or did not do to me, but I struggled to accept his seeming lack of interest in her life. Despite being a very wealthy man, he did nothing to contribute to her upbringing. Even before I became a Christian, I decided that if the circumstances were that I had to take a man to court to force him to support his own child, I would not do it.

In those early years, we managed by selling everything of value and by my going back to work. When I did become a Christian, God gave me a promise at a time when we were struggling financially, and I was considering asking Adrian for help. God said, "There is nothing he could give you that I cannot provide." I am so grateful for that promise, which time after time has proven to be true.

One specific occasion occurred early on in my Christian experience. During the year in which Dimity turned three, I obtained a full time, permanent teaching position with Education Queensland. Housing loan interest rates were at seventeen percent. Childcare fees were high, but I had managed to save enough for us to have a holiday at the end of the school year. We drove one thousand kilometres south to Wollongong to spend Christmas with my brother, John, and his family. I had then planned a few days in Sydney staying at a motel. Dimity and I spent a day at the famous Taronga Park Zoo, and we had two things left on our holiday wish list. I especially wanted to go on a cruise on Sydney Harbour and Dimity especially wanted to have a meal at McDonalds. It is hard to believe that there was a time in our lives when we had never eaten at maccas.

By now it was the New Year. I had been paid up until December 31 and went to the bank to withdraw money from the wages I was expecting had been deposited into my account. There was no deposit. There was no money. Thankfully, I had paid the motel bill and had filled the car with petrol. Now we only had twenty dollars cash to get us back home.

Disappointed, we went to a park on the north shore of Sydney Harbour, walked along the jetty and watched the boats, knowing that there would be no cruise. When a small ferry pulled in to the jetty, the driver asked me where we would like to go. I replied that we weren't going anywhere. Just looking. He seemed to sense our emotional state and made kind and unexpected offer.

"I do a circuit around the harbour, he said, "come on board and I will take you and your daughter for an hour's cruise."

We had a free tour of the harbour with all the sights, returning to our starting point decidedly happier than when we left.

As we walked back to our car, a man stopped us, lifted up the boot of his car and said, "Would you like some McDonalds?"

His boot was filled with burgers, fries, shakes and soft drinks. We couldn't believe our eyes. He explained that he had bought food for a family get together in the park but most of the people had pulled out at the last minute and that he was left with all of this McDonald's food. Dimity and I had a picnic in the park and also took food back to the motel with us. This set us in good stead for the long drive home.

God does know everything and His timing is perfect. I have never forgotten the provision of these two men in the right place at the right time offering us exactly what we desired but had no way of procuring it for ourselves.

God's greatest provision to me has been his very presence. Hearing the voice of God and experiencing outpourings of love and grace have transformed my very being. It is hard to imagine what life would have been like without this vital relationship.

I went back to teaching Physical Education when Dimity was fourteen months old. It was here that I crossed paths with one of Adrian's friends, who was now a representative for a sporting company. He told me that Adrian had remarried. That information consistently ate at me. I was fine when I was busy at home or at school, but when in the car by myself, I was consumed with anger, and even hatred. Thankfully those destructive emotions abated quickly when I was no longer alone.

I knew I could not allow those feelings to continue eating away at me so, counter to what I really was feeling, I rang him up and said, "I heard that you have married, and I just wanted to congratulate you."

I didn't mean a word of it, but I knew I had to take action and say it. Released from my negative emotions, I was able to get on with life without obsessing about him, and these destructive emotions gradually disappeared.

Shortly after this was when I had that first powerful

experience of church. The transformation of my life soon enabled me to forgive him from the heart and to genuinely wish him all the very best. Then I received complete healing and freedom.

When Dimity was eighteen, Adrian contacted me and asked to meet his daughter. I was unsettled and dubious, but Dimity had every right to decide for herself. When I told her of his request, she was mystified as to why, after eighteen years of neglect, he wanted to meet now. She also said she wanted to write him a letter, so he knew some things about her before they met. She let me read the letter and has allowed me to include some of her statements:

I want you to know that the most important person in my life is God. I won't do anything that disappoints God.

The second most important person in my life is my mother. I do not want my meeting you to hurt her in any way.

I want you to know that I have no hard feelings towards you and that I forgive you.

I felt proud of her when I read her letter and realised two things: one, that Dimity was more gracious than I was; two, that God had answered my prayer and given me a godly daughter.

I went with Dimity for the first two meetings for support and then withdrew. Adrian has remained a part of her life since that first meeting. Dimity was keen to introduce her husband-to-be Pete, to Adrian. A significant occasion occurred when Pete witnessed Adrian signing Dimity's birth certificate.

I was delighted to meet each of my four grandchildren just hours after their birth. To hold Indiana, Lee, Peyton and Austin as newborn babies gave me complete joy and peace. The journey of being a grandmother has taken me from cradling those newborns and singing them to sleep, to celebrating each and every milestone. Now we are going on adventures together, finding joy in expanding our comfort zones. They constantly fill my emotional tank, and I am so grateful to Dimity and my son-in-law, Pete, for giving me these opportunities to express my love.

25
Continuing to Embrace Life

Having retired from formal ministry, much of which had taken me away from family and friends for long periods of time, I was now delighted to be able to reconnect with these significant people.

Reconnecting with valued family and friends has brought me great joy since retiring. However, these two factors, retirement and renewed focus on relationships, had the potential to cause me to neglect the most important relationship of all. I accept that I have let Jesus down so many times. The purpose of my life has always been that somehow Jesus might be seen and experienced through me; I just did not realise that for such a long time. It has taken me seventy years to appreciate this purpose.

For this purpose to be realised, my life needed to be lost in His life. The Holy Spirit led me into ministry quite early in my Christian life. I relied on the Holy Spirit every step of the way. He enabled me to fight the good fight. He won each victory when the flesh challenged the spirit. He was my teacher, comforter and counsellor. Now that I was not in formal ministry, I still needed him. Not just to lead, guide and enable, not just to be the source of my life, He is so much more than almighty power available whenever we call.

He is the life-giving spirit. When He joins his life with our life, it is so that we may become one with Him. A new life is created. Christians should be the most spiritually alive people on the planet. The same spirit who raised Jesus from the dead lives in us, so that together with Him, we too may have resurrection life.

It is the person of the Holy Spirit who makes that possible. It can be hard to see the Holy Spirit as a person and relate to him as such. It seems easier to identify with God the Father and with God the Son, Jesus Christ. They have names, distinct roles and responsibilities. Unfortunately, only knowing The Holy Spirit by the definite article, it is harder to see Him as a person: the third person of the Trinity.

During my second year at Bible College, I became engrossed in a subject called 'Doctrine of the Holy Spirit'. As I read and attended classes, I realised I had not had the experiences I was reading about. I felt the lack of a moment-by-moment reality of The Holy Spirit in my daily life. I prayed to God earnestly seeking such a spiritual life, and He spoke to me through His Word: "In a few days you will be baptized with the Holy Spirit."[20] I claimed that promise, not knowing how or when it would be fulfilled.

Three days later we had a guest preacher at my church. He spoke on the baptism of the Holy Spirit and made an altar call at the end. I went forward for prayer and believed that God had fulfilled His promise. That moment years earlier, when I accepted Jesus as my Lord and Saviour, I was flooded with love and power; now, I experienced what I can only describe as a cleansing. There was a new determination within me to lead a life worthy of His calling and presence. I still did not understand all that was happening, but I had a renewed sense that my life was to be totally lost in His life, in order to be filled with the Holy Spirit.

It was beyond my comprehension then, to expect that somehow my life could demonstrate the life of Christ. Now, thirty-five years later, I understand that The Holy Spirit was not only given to me as a source of personal blessing. My life, totally lost in His, enabled me to experience abundant life. He produced within me the ability to preach at a moment's notice, pray for healing, cast out demons and overcome all sorts of obstacles. I am not saying that always I respond and react as I should. Like many others, I am still learning to be completely led by The Holy Spirit and continue to struggle to produce love, joy, peace, patience, kindness, goodness, faithfulness, gentleness and self-control. However, the greatest gift of all is not the fruit The Holy Spirit produces but His very presence. He is the gift.

I think back to when I went to Woodridge in 1991 to plant a church. I was completely ill prepared and inexperienced. Yet God built the church. I remember meeting with my District Board of Ministerial Development before commencing at Woodridge.[21] During the interview I expressed a desire to have *spiritual* people in the church. The room became silent very quickly, and it was clear I had not adequately communicated what I meant. There seemed to be a reluctance to talk about the work of The Holy Spirit and a fear of potential excesses on the spectrum of Pentecostalism.

Coming straight from Bible College I was not aware of any such dangers. As time has passed, what I am aware of however, is the danger of *not* embracing the third person of the Trinity.

Transformation began with my surrender of every aspect of my life to God, trusting Him and loving him. As the Holy Spirit directed my path a new way of living began.

Now that I have time to reflect on the journey of my life, I am overwhelmed with gratefulness that Jesus came into my life. When He came into my life and filled me with love and power, transformation began. It was not that I had been a miserable failure in life. Despite my unhealthy relationship with Adrian, I had been happy and successful.

However, the fighting spirit in me was reckless and self-serving until my acceptance of Jesus. I thought that the killer instinct was essential to be a successful athlete but was completely mistaken. There were athletes I long admired who were known for their good character as well as for their athletic achievements. One such person was John Landy. He was the second person ever to run under four minutes for the mile. What made him even more famous, was that he stopped during an Olympic qualifying race in 1952, to go back and help Ron Clarke, a young athlete who had fallen.[22] Landy recovered and went on to win the race and qualify for the Olympics. In contrast, my killer instinct was such that, if I were in a quest to win, I would not have given the fallen athlete a thought. I would have just seen this as an increase in my chances of winning. In other words, it was all about me. I was self-centred and selfish.

After praying for the first time in fifteen years, when Dimity was threatened prenatally, and then praying for survival on a daily basis, I knew I had to keep God *in* my life. I had no theological knowledge, no desire to go to church, and certainly no concept of sinfulness and salvation however, I knew enough to know that God had to be in my life and not kept on standby for my next crisis. I could have turned my back on Him once each crisis had passed, but it never occurred to me to leave Him out.

However, my willingness to completely surrender every aspect of my life was not instantaneous. My life before loving Jesus was marked by success, independence and satisfying achievements. I was a really happy person. Only when a problem was too big for me or someone else to handle, did I turn to God. He answered my prayers of desperation, so I continued to rely on him.

When I finally understood my need to surrender my life to Jesus and I was powerfully flooded with love and power, I started to think more of others and their welfare. An interesting result of that total surrender was empowerment. Not the personal power I had relied on my whole life, but the Holy Spirit's power. The irony of the Christian life is that it is only when you stop living for yourself, that you experience real fulfilment. Abundant life comes when Jesus fills your life. Living for Jesus in the power and guidance of the Holy Spirit is the most amazing adventure.

This adventure of life in union with God is ultimately for his benefit and purposes. We are benefactors of this flourishing and abundant life. But that does not seem to happen if we treat God as if He exists for our benefit. I have been in a church when a young woman bounded on to the platform for a time of prayer. She proceeded to scream at God. "God you can do better than this!" I cringed and felt grieved on God's behalf.

How could anyone think that, out of the nearly eight billion people on planet Earth, God's responsibility is to ensure one particular individual's wellbeing and success? Of course, the paradox is that God does care about our intimate details and needs. I have personally experienced His intimate touch and witnessed His amazing love for many individuals. His desire is that none should perish[23] and He does intervene in the life of individuals. However, His purposes are far greater than we realise.

A question has challenged me for many years. Is God there to answer my prayers, guide and protect me and fulfil the many promises I read of in His Word, or has

God revealed Himself to me, so that I would *completely surrender* my life, dying to myself on a daily basis, in order to allow His Spirit total control, come what may?

I think that I always knew the answer to that question, but each succeeding year and new experience has cemented my belief with ever-increasing joy. When we receive The Holy Spirit, He unites us with God so that His love is manifested in us. The reality of dying to self and of Jesus somehow living through me is the most beautiful picture of a purposeful life. It is not that I do not matter. It is that His ways are greater than my ways. Therefore, my daily choice to join my life with His allows me to live a life of purpose: His purpose.

26
Blessed Union

As I begin my eighth decade, I look back on my life and am amazed at the reality of Jesus' personal presence through the Holy Spirit. My experience of Jesus is as a result of His life, death and resurrection. The promises He made to us about the Spirit include "[You will be] clothed with power", "I will be with you always", "I will send him to you" and "When he, the Spirit of truth, comes, he will guide you into all truth."[24] These echo God's promise in the Old Testament, "I will put my Spirit in you."[25]

In modern thinking the spirit is often linked to energy and enthusiasm, and there is sometimes a quest or desire for a healthy spiritual life. But we cannot attain this on our own. Our spirit needs to be connected to God's spirit: the Holy Spirit. Here is where abundant life becomes a reality, and it has little or nothing to do with the physical or the material. As our spiritual life is renewed through connection with the Holy Spirit, our energy and enthusiasm become focused on God's life within us. Our healthy spiritual life can then nourish our soul and satisfy our physical and emotional desires.[26]

One of the happiest days of my life was when Dimity married Pete. Like most mothers and daughters, we had long chats about what it would be like when she had a boyfriend. One day I asked her, "How many boyfriends do you want to have in your life?" She thought about her answer and then replied, "One." I expressed my belief that God was keeping her for the one man who would be her husband. There is something so special and mystical about marriage. The marriage vows usher in a new creation. Ideally, every decision is made in light of what is best for the marriage, rather than in light of the potential for individual happiness for one of the marriage partners. It is no wonder that God uses marriage to demonstrate the profound mystery of the unity he desires.

When we are spiritually alive, there is a realisation that we are not an independent entity. We are united with God through His Holy Spirit and therefore can have constant fellowship with Him. The focus is not that God enhances my life, but rather that my life connects to God through the Holy Spirit. This is abundant life and His life can then flow through me. This flow then becomes the purpose of my life. The Holy Spirit unites with my spirit. He guides me, reveals His will to me and gives me discernment. This is not done merely for my sake but also for the sake of others and ultimately for God's will to be done. Together with God, is it possible for my life to somehow be a blessing to Him and make a difference to His kingdom?

It was the leading of the spirit that took me to that half night of prayer where I was impacted by stories regarding world mission. It was the spirit that responded to my declaration to God that if He ever called me anywhere that I would go, by calling me to go to district conference. It was the spirit that led me to go to Kingsley College within three months of that conference. It was at Kingsley College that I met people full of the Holy Spirit who changed my life, and it was where I encountered the fullness of the Holy Spirit for myself.

I began to understand that God's call on my life was a journey filled with "god incidence."

Why did I invite Rita to come with me across the city where she would come face to face with her painful past? Why did this still vulnerable lady open up to me about her life and the unreasonable guilt she felt? God wanted Rita to receive healing and to be delivered from the false shame she still carried.

When I was a pastor, I would pray and ask God who should I visit? Whilst being mindful not to overlook anyone, the Holy Spirit guided me as to the timing of visits unless there had been a prearranged meeting. It may well be that not everyone likes to receive an unexpected visit from their pastor, but I never received a complaint about turning up unannounced. Instead, these were times when the real challenges of life were often shared, and meaningful relationships developed from that.

When I first began to walk with Jesus and had a great desire to understand the Bible, I read to look for instructions. I wanted to do everything I could to please Him. I did not want to disappoint Him or cause Him pain. I think this was my natural response to falling in love. When my pastor advised me to also look for God's promises, I did not see the need at that time. God had already given me everything, how could I expect Him to give me more? Of course, I later understood Him to be correct in valuing the amazing promises of God. However, my initial desire was solely to please Him and to not expect anything more because He had already given me so much. It has taken time and experience to begin to understand the partnership that God desires with us.

I understand now that I can never live a life that completely pleases God and meets all his requirements of holiness. I have been told over and over again that it is possible not to sin. I am the one most aware of my own shortcomings and failures. What I *can* do is to surrender my life daily to be led, guided, fed and taught by the Holy Spirit.

Paul considered everything else to be a loss compared to "the surpassing value of knowing Christ Jesus my Lord".[27] This knowledge comes through the Holy Spirit. He is our helper, comforter, friend, teacher and guide. As He quickens and strengthens us in our innermost being, our character is influenced and developed along the lines of Christ's character. The Holy Spirit should win every award for being Top Influencer.

Jesus, however, did not come only to take the punishment for our sin and to deliver us from the power of sin, nor did He come only to work through us to show His love to humankind. He came to bring us back into fellowship with the divine life: to make us, in fact, partakers of the divine nature.

> His divine power has given us everything needed for life and godliness, through the knowledge of him who called us by his own glory and goodness. Thus he has given us, through these things, his precious and very great promises, so that through them you may escape from the corruption that is in the world because of lust and may become participants of the divine nature.[28]

When we receive the Holy Spirit, we are united with God so that God's love is manifested in us. The soul united to God by the indwelling Holy Spirit enables us to be one with Jesus. Our true purpose is not to be of use to God but to be one with God.

This relationship needs to be fed, to grow and to be reproducible. As is the case with any marriage, in the process of joining our life with God through his Spirit, true transformation takes place. It is God's grace that allows this to be realised; it is not my effort. But it *is* my desire and my request.

We present our life to God and choose not to conform to the patterns of this world. (Romans 12:2) He renews our mind with truth and revelation brought by the Holy Spirit. Then we will live a natural life, but with total dependence on Him, the third person of the Trinity. We relinquish the rights to our life, identify with the death and resurrection of Jesus, and live the abundant life for which He conquered the power of evil.

The destiny of my spiritual life is to have such identification with Jesus that I hear God and know that He hears me. God is where I belong. This is where I am unconditionally loved. The result of total surrender and abandonment to him is delight. I am no longer a human being trying to be godly; God's life is pouring through me. The purpose of my life becomes God's purposes alone.

If I can live in this way, with my life hidden in Christ, my passionate devotion to Jesus will grow and bring me deep satisfaction. When I spoke to God, many years in Amsterdam, I prayed for Dimity to be a godly woman. I wasn't praying for her to be morally pure. I was praying that she would know God in ever-increasing intimacy and join her life with His in blessed union. Of all the things that I would want and hope for her, this is the ultimate.

While it was a process of time and understanding for me to totally surrender myself to God, there was no such hesitation on God's part. When I invited God into my life, He did not give a part of Himself and then wait to see how I progressed before He gave me more of himself. He gave completely in the form of His Holy Spirit. It has taken me a long time to understand God's gift of Himself. He is my shield, my very great reward. United with Him, the oneness is only possible when I too give, not in part, but the whole of my life. My identity is *in Christ*.

27

No Condemnation

A good friend once confessed to me that, when she first met me, she did not know how to talk to me. When I asked why, she replied that it was because she had never met a *single mother* before.

It surprised me that being a single mother was how she chiefly identified me. Not only did I not wear the label single mother on my forehead, my identity was not formed by my marital status.

I had experienced judgmental treatment from doctors and chemists back in the 1980s whenever I had medical issues with either my infant daughter or myself. The assumption from the medical profession seemed to be a judgment of superiority in that if you were a single mother, you must have a low IQ.

I also had issues with employees of Centrelink. In the days when paper files were kept in manila folders, I was told, just before one Christmas, that my file had apparently gone missing The young person at the counter showed no interest, let alone compassion, as she informed me it would take weeks to start a new file and restore payments.

What caused me most distress, apart from knowing I could not buy Christmas presents for my family, was the feeling of sheer powerlessness. I simply did not matter.

When people are made to feel that they don't matter it can wound their soul. God knows this and wants to repair the damage.

Counter to the message the world was giving me at the time, God demonstrated to me that I mattered to Him. The way in which He welcomed me that first night I went to church, and the flood of His love that came into my life was the most powerful voice of all. I am so thankful that I made the decision to never stop listening to His voice and went home to find my grandmother's Bible. I am thankful that I have never stopped listening to His voice. I am also mindful that throughout my life, God had spoken to me. I needed to choose to listen.

The potential for me or anyone else, to flourish in a forgiven and fruitful life was made possible because God the Father, Son and Holy Spirit was willing to suffer beyond our comprehension.

We have some understanding of the physical torture that Jesus suffered before and during His crucifixion. Perhaps we can imagine some of his emotional suffering as He was betrayed, denied and abandoned, but it is my belief that these sufferings alone were not the reason He sweated drops of blood and pleaded with his Father for some other way. God in three persons, the blessed Trinity, was about to be torn apart.

This unimaginable suffering experienced by the Godhead was not undertaken lightly or without cost. This unique and extreme suffering was undertaken to make it possible for all who believe to be saved. God took our punishment. These moments in history were supreme acts of love. This love is demonstrated in John 3:16, which begins, "For God so loved the world." John 3:17 goes on,

"God did not send his Son into the world to condemn the world, but to save the world through him."

If God's whole purpose in sending Jesus was *not* to condemn us, it is hard to understand why Christians can sometimes be condemnatory, especially in their reactions to what they consider to be "sinful" behaviour. I did not doubt God's love for me and his acceptance of me. However, there were certainly times when I felt labelled and misunderstood within the church.

I certainly felt at home the first time I went to church as an adult, and every time afterwards. However, there have been a few occasions when I have been shocked by the attitudes of individuals. I say shocked rather than hurt. I was not hurt, just confused.

On one such occasion I was walking, talking and praying with a close Christian friend when she told me we should stop and pray for my daughter. I had returned from Kingsley and was ministering in Woodridge, and I was not aware of any specific prayer need Dimity had. Then came the bombshell. We should pray for her, my friend said, because she had inherited my sin.

What was my sin? I had had an intimate relationship with a man I loved for ten years. Was that my sin? I had borne his child. Was that my sin? We hadn't been legally married. Was that my sin? I hadn't had an abortion. Surely, that couldn't be my sin?

I could not believe that my daughter would be punished for my sin. I was shocked by my friend's suggestion. My understanding of theology, still forming though it was, made me believe that Jesus died on the cross for my sin and that it had all been forgiven. No record had been kept of my wrongdoing. Jesus had taken it away. God looked at me as if I had not sinned. To me, atonement and justification were more than theological terms. They were my reality. I had been set free. I was loved and accepted and united with God. It is not my belief that our children inherit our sin or are punished for particular things we have done.

I was only too aware of many things I had done, that to my mind were far worse than having a committed relationship which included loving sex and which resulted in the birth of a child. If my daughter was, and I couldn't accept that she would be, somehow to be punished, surely it would be for *all* of my sin, not just for one sin deemed particularly bad because it was visible.

She may have suffered the consequences of my actions by growing up without a father, but she received so much more from her Heavenly Father. She received the knowledge that God intervened to give her life and she grew up with a mother who loved God with an open heart.

Many years later, as part of my preparation to go to the mission field, I was sent to a Christian counsellor for a psychological evaluation. When I arrived at her house, the first thing she wanted me to do was to meet her husband. I didn't think that was unusual until she said, "He has never met an ordained woman before and wants to see what one looks like." That interaction did not fill me with confidence. I was ordained in September 1992, more than a year after starting the church in Woodridge. In the fifteen years that followed, I never met anyone who thought an ordained woman was an oddity.

Worse was to come. Early in the interview, while filling out the forms, it naturally became apparent that I had a daughter but had never been married. I have never been ashamed of that fact. Being an unmarried mother has never embarrassed me. Then I got a response I did not expect.

Many years ago, I had almost lost a job because of my marital status. I had interviewed well and even gone to the school and taken lessons to demonstrate my expertise. I had verbally been offered the job. I had not mentioned that I was a single mother, because it was not primarily how I identified myself. I did not purposely hide that information; it just had not seemed relevant on a professional resumé. One of my referees mentioned to the potential employer how well he thought I had done bringing up my daughter on my own. No more questions were asked. That information was enough for them to consider not employing me. Could they possibly have such a person at their Christian school? I was asked to come in for a second interview so that this matter could be discussed.

This counsellor had a similar reaction. She plonked her pencil down on the desk, sat bolt upright with arms folded and boldly asked, "How, then, can you be an ordained minister?" I sat there thinking: Do you have no understanding of the grace of God? I didn't answer her question but simply completed the required questionnaire without giving her evaluation of me any credence.

It has been challenging for me to see how Christians react to a pregnancy outside marriage. I am aware of one instance, for example, where a young couple who were dating, went to their senior pastor to confess their sin and resulting pregnancy and were told they had two choices, abortion or marriage. This, to me, indicates that the underlying issue can sometimes be more about shame, embarrassment and saving face.

In contrast, being a single mother in Woodridge was no cause for shame. In fact, I was accepted as a real person and a valued member of society with a voice worth listening to. I never felt any judgment from the school, the local council with which I worked closely, or any member of the community. However, I constantly met people who thought they were too sinful to set foot inside a church. I have mentioned a time when one man said to me, "I have broken every one of the Ten Commandments." This is not the only time I heard this sentiment. When such people somehow developed enough trust to come to church and experienced love and acceptance there, it gave me the greatest joy.

Another incident that gave me great joy occurred when Dimity was seven years old. One Sunday she came home from Sunday school and excitedly told me what she had learned. "Mum, do you know what I realised this morning? Jesus is just like me. His parents weren't married when Mary got pregnant. So, He knows exactly how I feel, and He loves me."

There has only ever been one child born who was condemned before conception. That was Jesus Christ, our Lord and Saviour. That is what we are talking about when we read, "God gave his one and only Son."[29] Because He was willing to condemn His own son, no one else ever need be condemned.

Every person has the potential to be connected to God in an intimate way, through the death and resurrection of Jesus and the indwelling of the Holy Spirit. Our determination to be identified with Jesus does not mean that there will not be battles to fight and difficult races to run. However, I know only too well the need to be strong and courageous. We have the greatest coach who ever lived, and He is not standing on the sidelines cheering us on. He is in the battle; He is in the boxing ring, and in the race with us. He has already been crowned champion. When we are confident of our identity in Christ through the indwelling Holy Spirit, then the weapons of our battles are primarily love, grace, mercy and forgiveness. Having experienced God's amazing grace, I totally trust in what God's grace can do for you.

28

Don't Let the Fire Go Out

Fire that comes from above is much more than symbolic. After the Exodus God instructed his people, in regard to life and worship and He sent fire from heaven to burn on the altar. It was the role of the priests to ensure that the fire never went out.

At the Pentecost festival after Jesus had ascended to Heaven, individual flames of fire rested upon each of the disciples and they were filled with the Holy Spirit. From this moment on, they spoke and acted as the Holy Spirit enabled them and the church was born.

When the flame of the Holy Spirit descends upon us, this fire, although symbolic, is meant to be all consuming. We present the entirety of our life and choose not to live according to the pattern of the world. God transforms by the renewing of our mind. He gives us a different mindset and our way of thinking is continually being renewed by the Holy Spirit.

To keep the fire of the Holy Spirit burning within us, we need the same passion that Paul talks about when he declares that above all, he wants to know Christ. God fans the flame every minute we spend with Him. Other likeminded Christians also add kindling to the fire. Worshipping together is like sitting around a bonfire and being warmed deeply in the soul.

It is interesting that the term often used when there is a state of emotional, physical and mental exhaustion is "burnout." This word is equally applied to those in Christian service who simply cannot go on. The fire has gone out. It may have been put out by strong winds of resistance or storms of opposition or it may have been neglected. Neglect may not even be intentional. It may come from sheer exhaustion. If I am unable to stoke the fire in my own life, then we rely on other members of the body of Christ to share their fire. Remember when, on my first trip to Mono, our team of five was left to their own resources, the first thing Dorah did was to visit neighbours and get fire from them. She carried that fire in a half coconut shell and the fire was not allowed to go out.

After the third home invasion in Woodridge, my spiritual tank was empty. During the oppression of working under a toxic boss in Australia, I was exhausted emotionally. When I left Solomon Islands I was certainly spent physically. In all of these circumstances, it was the prayers of those who cared for me that carried me through.

There is enormous power in a strong team of prayer supporters. I shared openly with my team and I knew that they were faithful, not only praying for me but also praying for the people God was bringing into my life.

I will never know all of the people who prayed for me at various times, but I am forever grateful for each one. I drew great comfort from the knowledge that their prayers were not necessarily dependent upon my communication with them. An example would be when I was incapacitated with malaria. The impetus for prayer came not from me but from The Holy Spirit. It was the relationship that individuals in my prayer team had with God that was far more important than the relationship they had with me. I had over one hundred prayer partners throughout my time in Woodridge. Many of those were also on my prayer team throughout my years in Solomon Islands. People throughout Australia who were faithful in their prayer support joined them. Unfortunately, when I was ministering in established local churches, I did not enlist a force of prayer warriors. Perhaps I was unaware of the challenges I would face and took those ministries for granted. I am thankful for the Christian counsellor who reminded me of the spiritual resources available to me and urged me to make the relationship with God my priority.

The times when we cannot find the strength, or find the words to say, the Body of Christ can rekindle the flame for us. During the years I lived and ministered in Woodridge, I expected to be there for the rest of my life. Similarly, when I was in Solomon Islands, I had not thought of being anywhere else. To me, the strongest remedy against burnout is the total assurance that you are where God wants you to be. This is what ultimately led me to persevere throughout all the challenges at Woodridge.

I had so much to learn and am still learning. The process of dying to self is a painful and costly one. I was so easily offended and had such a strong sense of justice and of my "rights." I was concerned about my reputation and of perceptions of my success or failure. I am so thankful for every person and every opportunity given me to recognise these areas of my life that had to change. I am sure there are still many more necessary adjustments to be made. It seems to me that every time I insist on my "rights", I detract from Jesus, who totally surrendered his rights for me.

I absolutely trust in what Jesus has done for me and in what The Holy Spirit continues to do in me. I also trust God's grace, motivated by his love, to completely fulfil any life surrendered to him. The Holy Spirit set my life ablaze. There were times when I allowed the struggles and challenges of ministry to almost extinguish the fire, however, the bellows God used to fan the embers was my Christian brothers and sisters. I am forever grateful to dwell with you in the family of God.

End Notes

1. Cuts was the term commonly used for getting the cane. School Principals were allowed to use a cane to discipline students. Boys usually received their punishment across their hands while girls more often received their punishment on their legs.

2. Portable chemical toilet

3. John 10:16 *New International Version.*

4. Queensland schools call their canteens, tuckshops.

5. This is a method of cooking food using heated rocks buried in a pit oven.

6. Genesis 24:27 *King James Version,*

7. Solomon Islands is the correct name for the country and therefore the definite article is not necessary. However, the country is often referred to as 'the Solomons'.

8. Jeremiah 12:5.

9. Wood, A. Harold. *Overseas Mission of the Australian Methodist Church*, Vol. 2, Melbourne: Aldersgate Press, 1975, pp. 148–49.

10. Luxton,C.T.J. *Isles of Solomon*. Wellington, New Zealand: Methodist Foreign Society of New Zealand. 1955.

11.Luxton p. 44.

12. Luxton p. 47-49.

13. Luxton p. 51.

14. Centrelink is the Australian Government agency that determines eligibility for income support and is responsible for the delivery of that support to those who are found to be eligible.

15. Betel nut is a large nut, which when chewed, can have psychoactive effects. It was traditionally chewed by tribal elders before making decisions, but in more recent times has become very popular amongst all age groups. It is known to have addictive qualities and is therefore advocated against by the church.

16. Matthew 28:18–20 (NRSV).

17. Acts 2:38 (NRSV).

18. Parker, Percy Livingstone (ed.). *The Journal of John Wesley*, Chicago: Moody Press, 1951, entry for 14 February 1736.

19. Luxton, *Isles of Solomon*, p. 44.

20. Acts 1:5.

21. In the Wesleyan Methodist Church, the DBMD monitors, encourages and directs candidates towards ordination or other categories of recognised ministry.

22. Roger Bannister ran 3.50.4 for the mile on May 6, 1954. John Landy ran 3.57.9 on 21 June 1954. Ron Clarke lit the flame for the 1956 Melbourne Olympics and went on the break seventeen world records as a distance runner.

23. Second Peter 3:9.

24. Luke 24:49; Matthew 28:20 (GNT); John 16:7; John 16:13.

25.Ezekiel 36:27.

26. Ephesians 6:31,32,

27. Philippians 3:8 (NRSV).

28. Second Peter 1:3, 4 (NRSV).

29. John 3:16.

Acknowledgements

I was recently asked how long it had taken me to work on this book. After I had replied that it had been close to three years, I realised that in fact it is a work of seventy years.

Thank you to everyone who has sown into my life throughout all of those years. Some are named in the book but most are not. I am grateful to everyone whom I have had the privilege to call friend. I am also grateful for everyone who has at one time or another, been opposed to me in some way. Every interaction has been valuable and necessary. I love you all.

I especially want to thank specific people who have made the completion of this book possible. Firstly, my editor, Owen Salter and, secondly, my unofficial editor, friend and confidant, Julie Tyler. You are the only one whose confrontation I enjoy. Jai Greenaway has given me many hours of her valuable time and expertise. Jai, your wisdom has been invaluable. Thanks and appreciation also to Jeanette O'Hagan for her formatting and practical expertise.

About the Author

Kay Fulcher is a retired pastor who has lived a vibrant and exciting life in ministry. She is a teacher turned pastor, turned missionary to Solomon Islands, where she served for seven years. Now semi-retired, Reverend Kay still writes, preaches and teaches when given the opportunity to do so.

Her life has taken her to many different places and people giving her a wide missionary perspective and a heart for those who don't know Jesus.

Web Address: https://www.allfiredupstories.com.au/

www.ingramcontent.com/pod-product-compliance
Lightning Source LLC
Chambersburg PA
CBHW032015050726
47590CB00006B/2182